Flower Arranging for Shows

Mary Napper

B T Batsford Ltd London

Dedication

To the many members of the National Association of Flower Arrangement Societies whom I am privileged to call my friends, and without whose help over the years this book would not have been possible.

First published 1984
© Mary Napper 1984

ISBN 0 7134 4053 8

Printed in Great Britain
by The Anchor Press Ltd
Tiptree, Essex
for the publishers,
B.T. Batsford Ltd,
4 Fitzhardinge Street,
London W1H 0AH

Contents

ACKNOWLEDGEMENTS

I would like to thank Mrs Betty Treweeke, chairman of the judging committee of the National Association of Flower Arrangement Societies; Mrs Valerie Humphries, vice-chairman of the education committee of the National Association of Flower Arrangement Societies; Mrs Mavis Brooker; Mr Ron Davies; Dr Ken Loveday; Mrs Catherine Pettit; Mr David Saunders; Mr Derek Smith; and the many flower arrangers who have kindly allowed me to use photographs of their exhibits.

I am grateful to Mr Timothy Auger of B.T. Batsford Ltd for his help and advice; and last but by no means least to my husband for his encouragement and patience.

List of Illustrations

All photographs are authentic exhibits staged at competitive shows or Festivals.

Introduction

As flower arranging has given a new purpose to gardening so has showing given a new purpose to arranging flowers. Few arrangers take their friends on a tour of the garden in order to point out a bed of this or a mass of that, but introduce them instead to a plant whose leaves are invaluable in many arrangements, or one which has beautiful seed heads. Shrubs are grown for their attractive foliage; flowers for their off-beat colours. However limited is our love of gardening all flower arrangers will find the inclination, the time, and indeed the space to pop in that special plant, whether it is a cutting from the demonstrator's rubbish box, or purchased from a sales table at a show or garden centre.

Design in our flower arranging has influenced design in our gardens. Gone are the rows of wall flowers and bulbs, followed by annuals. Instead we have beds planted according to the size and shape of leaves or with foliage colour in mind. Well, that was the intention, but sometimes we find that having discovered the ideal spot for a particular plant which we have always wanted because 'it is such good outline material' or because its colour would be 'so useful for transition', our well-laid plans have gone awry, resulting in the survival of the fittest. With our show work we must be more disciplined, and 'if in doubt leave out'. We should not be tempted to use a piece of foliage because we have grown it from a cutting and are feeling very proud of it. Take it home – enjoy it at home.

When we enter a show we are demonstrating our skills and ability not just to our friends but for all to see how we use the plant material which we have grown with much care and attention. Shows have been enjoyed by many for several decades. Every town and village organizes its own summer show and there is nearly always a class for flower arranging. Why are they still popular? Why do we wish to enter a show? What makes us want to compete? Is it for the trophy or cup which we might win? I hope not. If we are lucky enough to win a prize, it is a 'little extra'. Our real reward is gained from the improved standard in our work, the enjoyment, experience and excitement, and for the friends we make during the show.

As our flower arranging opens our eyes to the beauty around us, show work broadens our knowledge in so many fields from which inspiration comes. We become more aware of artists in other spheres; how great painters balance colour, form and shape; how sculptors use space and texture. Interpreting the schedule requires research so we come to appreciate the writings of authors, playwrights and poets. Pages of history come alive. Many of us when arranging flowers in our homes continually use the same containers, put our flowers in the same positions and use similar plant material. Our flower arranging has become almost automatic and has lost inspiration. Showing will prevent this happening.

Arranging for show work whether competitive or for exhibition, is quite different from doing the flowers at home. It will make you experiment with different styles, different plant material and different colours regardless of whether they are suitable for your own home. You will achieve a higher standard of work by competing with the more proficient and by comparing your standard with others. At home you have only your own arranging as a yardstick. You will come to accept, to learn from and appreciate the constructive criticisms of the judges.

Flower arranging like art is progressive, therefore rules and styles change, but basic principles remain the same. You may ask whether there is any need for rules in flower arranging, or even if it should be competitive. Yes, competition is good for us and our work, and if it is competitive then there must be rules by which it is judged. Competition acts as a stimulant, urging us to do our best, to try harder and pay more attention to detail. It provokes new thoughts and increases our knowledge in many subjects.

Shows are meeting grounds for people with a common interest, whether they are competitors or spectators. They are particularly valuable to the less experienced flower arranger who wishes to improve her standard. Much can be learned by discussing her exhibit with the more experienced competitor and exchanging ideas on mechanics, backgrounds, drapes and growing plant material.

Each society and show has its rules by which it is judged and competitors should ensure they are familiar with the current set before planning their exhibits. A large number of horticultural, Women's Institute and county shows are judged according to the latest edition of the *Handbook of Schedule Definitions* published by the National Association of Flower Arrangement Societies, and are judged by qualified judges belonging to, and trained by NAFAS. The majority of schedules are compiled using the terminology suggested in the Associations schedule definitions.

Throughout this book continuous reference will be made to flower clubs and to terms used by flower arrangers. Who are these flower arrangers? The vast majority are members of one of the 1,400 flower clubs throughout Great Britain which form the National Association of Flower Arrangement Societies. There is almost certainly a flower club near you. If your interest in flower arranging has been stimulated and you wish to develop it further, suggestions as to how you may achieve this are given later on.

The intention of this book is not to teach the principles of good flower arranging. It is designed to help competitors and show organizers, whether they are part of a horticultural show which includes classes for flower arranging or a flower club, by providing information about practical details. Consequently, subjects such as balance, scale and harmony are touched upon briefly but not in depth.

With no disrespect to the many talented men now involved in flower arranging but merely to eliminate the continuous use of 'he/she' and 'him/her', the feminine gender has been used throughout this book.

My aim has been to share with you the knowledge I have gained whilst being involved with competitive and non-competitive shows. If you the competitor, exhibitor or member of a show committee find this book useful my object will have been achieved.

1. Planning the Show

ELECTING THE COMMITTEE

You have decided to hold a show. Well done, but in order to stage a show an organizing committee of approximately ten people (depending on the size of the show and what you intend to include) should be formed. These should include a chairman who should preside at all meetings; a show secretary; a treasurer; a competition secretary; stewards; and people to look after staging; printing and publicity; hospitality; and sales tables.

First we will consider the requirements for the show before explaining the duties of each committee member.

CHOOSING THE VENUE AND DATE

At your first meeting you should decide on the venue, date, timing and an overall title which sets the theme for the show. This should not be too restricting because the classes you stage should all relate to it. If you are an inexperienced group planning your first show, remember that small is beautiful. A carefully organized, well staged small show will be far more attractive and satisfying than a disorganized, badly staged larger one.

Choose your venue carefully. Sometimes your choice of halls is limited. If you do have a choice, decide on one which is not so large that your exhibits are lost and it looks half empty even when the public are admitted, nor so small that it is too crowded for the public to be able to see your work in comfort.

When deciding upon a date, consideration should be given to any other local events planned for the same time as this might reduce the attendance. If it is too near Mothering Sunday, Easter, or St Valentines' Day, florists' flowers may be slightly more expensive and certain colours and varieties will probably be scarce such as lillies at Easter and red flowers for St Valentine's Day. It is advisable to avoid the summer holiday season as competitors and visitors may be away from home. Children at home on school holidays do not always make it easy for parents to be occupied with staging, entering and attending a show.

BOOKING A JUDGE

Your entries need judging, therefore a judge must be booked. If you are an affiliated club of NAFAS you will have an area and national list of qualified judges. If you are a branch of the Women's Institute or part of a horticultural society, enquiries regarding judges may be made to the headquarters of the National Association of Flower Arrangement Societies. There will usually be a member of your society who is connected with the flower arranging world and who will help you obtain the name of a qualified judge, if you wish the show to be judged according to the NAFAS *Handbook of Schedule Definitions*.

INVITING YOUR GUESTS

You may decide to invite a local personality or an officer of your association to open the show and later to present the prizes. Both travelling expenses and hospitality should be offered and it is a nice gesture to present her with a small basket or arrangement of flowers as a token of appreciation.

DEALING WITH EXPENSES

At this stage you will need some money for staging material, duplicating, printing and publicity, with the rental of the hall, prize money and judges expenses coming later. Regard this as a loan or float because you will soon be receiving entry fees from competitors, then entrance money at the door, money from the raffle or tombola and any of the other money raising tables you have organized.

ORGANIZING THE SALES TABLES

On the day the competitors stage their exhibits, you will need to have a mechanics' sales table to include such items as pinholders, water retaining foam, scissors, stub wires, reel wire and cones (especially if a pedestal class is included in the schedule) available just in case, in their nervousness, competitors have left one or other of these items sitting on their door steps.

If you have plenty of visitors to the show you must keep them interested then they will come again. Try to include well staged stalls selling the ever popular homemade cakes and preserves, plants which have been donated by your members, items such as bookmarks, blotters and correspondence cards, all made with dried or pressed plant material.

Run a tombola or raffle. Serve teas with homemade cakes and scones. Man an information table from which potential members can obtain particulars of the club or society's activities, such as the dates and times of meetings and details of forthcoming events. Display photographs from previous events.

ALLOCATING DUTIES

With all this to organize and only ten people to do it, what is the best way of allocating the various duties? Some members will probably be more experienced than others. The newer members, who are the show committee officers of tomorrow, can tackle jobs such as organizing the raffle or tombola, and looking after the sales tables and hospitality, whilst those with show experience can assume the role of competition secretary, taking charge of the staging, or handle publicity.

The chairman
This is the person responsible for the overall organization of the show. She takes the chair at all the committee meetings and should be aware of everything that is being planned for the show by other members of the committee. She is responsible for drafting agendas, approving draft minutes before circulation, and acting on the minutes unless otherwise stated. She should receive and entertain any guests such as the show's opener, local personalities, officers of the association, club or society, and escort them around the show. When the show is over she should send the very important letters of thanks to the committee, helpers and judges.

The secretary
She should circulate agendas for, and take minutes of, all meetings, and attend to the general correspondence. She should confirm the booking of the hall or marquee as well as the judges. At the show she should be ready to answer all enquiries made at the Information table. If you feel the size of your show warrants it, an invitation should be sent to either the Red Cross or St John's Ambulance Service to attend.

The treasurer
She is responsible for all finances including committee travelling expenses, postage and telephone, paying the judge's expenses and arranging any necessary insurance. On the day of the show she must ensure the prize money is ready in envelopes clearly marked with the class and award and that floats are available for such items as raffle, stalls, teas. She should also take the entrance money at the door.

The competition secretary

This is a very responsible job. The competition secretary should work closely with the member who prepares the hall and tabling for the competitors, but for smaller shows she may undertake the staging herself. She is responsible for preparing the schedule and producing the first draft, so it is helpful if she can type. She is responsible for sending a copy of the schedule to the judge before it is printed, duplicated and circulated. She will also deal with the acceptance of entries and entry fees from the competitors.

Her other duties include collecting prior to the show the challenge cups and trophies from the previous winners and cleaning them. She will also need to obtain any other class awards together with award cards and first-, second- and third-prize stickers. She will allocate the positions where the competitors' entries are to be staged and set out the competitors' cards.

She should make a list of prizewinners available for the press, the chairman, and whomever is presenting the cups and trophies. For the prizegiving ceremony she will need to make certain that all trophies, prizes and prize monies are to hand, and that receipts giving their names and addresses are obtained from the winners of the challenge cups and trophies which are awarded annually.

Staging

The person responsible for this must be meticulous and work closely with the competition secretary. She should help her prepare the schedule giving the number of classes, the number of entries to be staged in each class, and the type and style of classes to be included.

Space for sales and information tables, non-competitive exhibits (if any), catering and first aid facilities must be taken into consideration before deciding on the number and size of entries you can stage. You must allow sufficient space for the viewing public, remembering that it is space for competitive entries you need rather than for sales tables, however much of an asset the latter may prove to be. It is a competitive flower arranging show first and foremost.

Ensure that there is sufficient tabling, that staging for the hanging class is firm, and the staging is the correct height (4 ft 6in.; 1.37m.) for miniatures and petites.

If you are a small horticultural society, a branch of the Women's Institute or a newly affiliated flower club and are organizing a competitive show for the first time, your staging material will be an expensive item. Approach your nearest flower arranging club, having obtained the address from the local library. It may be willing to hire out material or niches to encourage you to get started. If you do have this valuable help, make sure the material is clean and dry when you return it.

Printing and duplicating

This job may be coupled with publicity as the printing is usually almost complete before publicity becomes too demanding. All printing and duplicating should be undertaken by one committee member. This is to ensure there is consistency in colour, type and information.

Your printing requirements will differ according to the size of the show and money available, but whether printed, photocopied or duplicated, stationery and publicity material should all be kept as simple and uncluttered as possible. It is facts which people are looking for. If you decide on printing, get an estimate first, and to avoid errors insist on seeing proofs.

However small your show, you will require schedules, entry forms, competitors' class cards and award cards. You may also like to obtain handbills which are so useful for sending to other local organizations, and for advertising in shop windows. Shops prefer handbills as they take up less window space than posters. If you are running more than one ancillary event such as a demonstration, preview, or luncheon, you will need tickets in order to sell them in advance. It is advisable to use a different colour for each event.

Posters should always be well produced and eye-catching with the minimum of lettering giving maximum of detail: what, where, and who if you have a well-known personality attending who will be an attraction. Also include any special features. Exhibitors passes, car stickers and badges for the committee should all be considered.

The same colour should be used for all printing, and if the schedule and entry forms are duplicated, coloured paper could be the same colour as the staging material and stewards' sashes, giving consistency throughout.

Publicity

This is vital if you are to attract competitors and the viewing public. Publicity before the show is far more important than during, because it will bring in the people and could result in an increase in club membership. Enthusiasm for what you are doing is one of the best forms of publicity. Chairmen and other committee members should bubble with enthusiasm for their wonderful show. Enthusiasm is catching and makes other people want to be part of what you are doing.

Involve your local press in the show by putting an advertisement in your local paper. This makes the press aware of the event, and they are more likely to cover the show especially if, when sending in your pre-show copy feature with a request for a photographer to attend, you remind them that you have taken paid advertisement space, and are not just expecting free publicity from them.

A flower show is no longer news. You must have something different to attract publicity. It is people who make news so if you can feature a local person, such as a club member, your show will stand more chance of getting into print. Photographs which are published after the event will help your next show. If the press are expected, they should be met by the publicity officer who should not only have the results available, but should have a press release ready giving details of the club or society, such as when and where it meets, and any special features of the show.

Your local shops will often publicize your show especially if an attractive arrangement is used, incorporating a small poster, handbill or car sticker. Do not be tempted to use fresh flowers unless you are prepared to keep them perfectly fresh. They rarely last for more than two days in shop windows which tend to be hot and very dry. If you stick your small poster or handbill to card and frame this with dried plant material, placing it on a plate stand, you have an attractive and acceptable advertisement. Your local newsagent may be prepared, for a small fee, to deliver your handbills with the papers.

Local radio stations are often looking for forthcoming events to include in their local events spot. Contact them four or five weeks before the show takes place giving them basic details: type of event, venue, time, day, date. Then send a reminder two or three weeks later. The radio spot should come as close to your show as possible. You may also wish to contact the AA or RAC for direction signs.

You might also obtain the address of the secretaries of the local flower clubs, womens' and church organizations and horticultural societies, and send them a handbill or circular letter together with a schedule so that they have all the details about the show.

Stewards
Whatever the size of your show stewards play a vital part in the smooth running of the event. They should be easily distinguishable by means of a sash or badge. On staging day they should help competitors into the hall with their equipment informing them where water may be obtained, and where boxes and belongings may be left until dismantling.

Prior to the show the stewards should be well briefed as to the position of each class, where the exits and toilets are situated, and where refreshments may be obtained. During the show they should know where the Best in Show entry is staged and ensure the exhibits are not touched.

Raffle or tombola

Whoever looks after this should find out first whether raffles are allowed in the hall. A licence will need to be obtained if tickets are sold in advance, otherwise cloakroom tickets are adequate.

The advantage of a tombola is that prizes are collected on the spot, so they don't have to be posted to the winners. Whereas, if a raffle is drawn towards the end of the show after some of the visitors have left, then prizes have to be sent on to them.

Judges' steward

This committee member should work closely with the competition secretary. Before judging starts she should check that each entry card is placed face downwards covering the competitor's name, and that all competitors have left the hall or marquee. She should make certain that the judge has everything she might need, and should have with her a schedule, tape measure, pen, a class list on which to record the results, award stickers (first, second, third, etc.) which should only be fixed after the class has been completely judged. She should inform the judge where each class is situated and how many entries it has. She should remain in the background whilst judging is taking place, speaking only when asked for information. She should ensure that any trophies are awarded correctly.

Hospitality

There is usually no difficulty in finding somebody to undertake this job with a few friends, because somehow flower arranging and food seem to go together. Very few flower arrangers are poor cooks. People for whom refreshment is to be provided should be decided well in advance and may include some or all of the following: the show opener, the presenter of prizes, the committee and the judges. When a judge arrives at the show, a welcoming cup of coffee is always appreciated, as are light refreshments after judging has been completed.

Stall holders usually appreciate a cup of tea being taken to them, or having a member of the committee take over for a while so that they can obtain their own refreshments. A table should be reserved for the workers.

Tea and coffee may also be served to the general public.

2. Setting the Scene

CHOOSING THE VENUE

Hiring the hall

When making preliminary enquiries about hiring a hall, the first thing to establish is the cost and whether there are any extras, such as use of electricity including spotlights or the use of the stage and kitchen. You will also need to know:

1 Exactly what is covered by the owner's insurance, such as public liability, personal injury, fire, loss or damage to property, or whether you need to take additional cover.
2 The fire regulations governing the hall which must be adhered to. You may need to fireproof the fabric used for your staging.
3 Whether there are tables or any other equipment which could be used for staging.
4 Whether the car parking facilities are adequate.
5 The extent of the catering facilities (availability and amount of crockery, tea urns, etc.)
6 Whether you are permitted to run a raffle or tombola. Halls attached to some churches are not permitted to be used for this form of lottery.

As soon as possible after your decision has been made, you should measure the exact size of the hall with all details, otherwise, when making the schedule, if you do not know exactly how much space you have, it will be difficult to decide on the type of staging, the number of classes and number of entries in each class and how much room you have left to accommodate your sales tables.

Planning your space

Plan on graph paper. Measure the length and width of hall, marking the distance from corners to any doors, indicating which way they open and whether they are fire exits and therefore must be left clear. Also note the position and size of windows and recesses, and any other appendages on the walls which might interfere with your staging such as protruding radiators, pillars, electric light brackets, etc.

Be sure to measure your stage and entrance hall. Note whether the steps from the stage protrude into the hall and if these are easily negotiable, whether the floor of the stage slopes, whether there are spotlights along the front and also the colour of the curtains, then decide whether it would be practical to use the stage for a class or whether it would be better to keep it for the prize-giving. Mark the position of electric light and spotlight switches and also electric points.

Measure the height, width, and length of tables. It is surprising how often these vary slightly especially in height. Find out how many are available.

Marquees

You may be using a marquee which is not quite as easy or practical as a hall, especially if the ground is not very even; you must therefore be prepared to do some levelling of tables with pieces of wood inserted under the legs.

The ground is invariably damp because the canvas draws the moisture up, so allow a space of at least two inches between the bottom of your table skirting and the ground, otherwise the skirting will act as blotting paper and it will soon become very damp.

The weather is always difficult to predict. In case of wet weather it is advisable to budget for duckboards at the entrance and matting inside to prevent the aisles becoming too muddy. Hopefully you will not require them, but it is better to be safe than sorry. Nothing is worse, especially for the committee who are on duty all day, than squelching mud.

Deciding on size

The size of your hall obviously dictates the size of your show and the number of classes you can put into your schedule, according to the type of staging you use, and also the number of entries in each class. Do not be tempted to squash in too many. Go for comfort and quality rather than quantity.

When you have estimated the number of entries you can comfortably stage in each class, bearing in mind the average entry is 2 ft 6 in. (75 cm.) wide, cut out your staging to scale from another sheet of graph paper, class by class, and juggle it around on your basic plan until you have a pleasing layout. Members of the public appreciate a floral spectacle to greet them as they walk into the hall, not the back of a row of niches, or the cake stall which may look very tempting when the show first opens but it is very depressing when it is empty at the end of the first hour.

Try to stage a complete class altogether. Think of the judges. It is very disconcerting to walk from one end of the hall to the other judging the same class because it has been split. If, for instance, a class of miniatures or petites are staged on two round tables, one at one end of the hall, the other at the other end, it is not only difficult for the judges to compare exhibits but also bewildering for the public who may see the first and third prizewinners on one table and then have to look for the second at the other end of the hall.

Staging against windows is often unavoidable because of space, but it restricts the light because backgrounds will be needed, so if possible arrange your line of tables at an angle to the window, allowing if possible an isle of 6 ft (1.8 m.) between the rows of exhibits.

Allowance must also be made for whatever sales tables you have decided to include, but bear in mind that it is a competitive show and priority must be given to accommodating your entries even if it means forfeiting a money-raising table.

When staging a winter show you have the problem of avoiding the radiators unless the heat can be turned off. If this is impossible, try to stage classes of fresh material as far away from the radiators as possible to prevent plants from wilting.

The staging

This can include tabling with backgrounds or niches, individual platforms raised 8 or 9 in. (20 or 22 cm.) from the floor, individual tables for table settings, pedestals, or hanging arrangements staged on peg boards. If the staging is raised it is more interesting for the competitors, and will give a far less monotonous look than rows of tabling. It is possible to use the front of the stage. Do not be put off if it has spotlights along the front. Miniatures and petites, which should be staged at a height of 4 ft 6 in. (1.45 m.) can be raised over and above these by using planks on bricks or trestle table tops on beer or milk crates, and then covering them with fabric.

Look at your plan. Look at your schedule. Visualize the show when staged. Have you variety in your staging? Have you allowed sufficient room between classes for the public to view in comfort without causing any bottlenecks? Have you sited your sales tables which are likely to sell out quickly, e.g. cakes and plants, in a convenient position to enable them to be removed when empty?

PREPARING THE STAGING

Selecting your fabric

Most of your staging whether it is tabling or individual platforms will require covering in fabric. However enthusiastic and imaginative you are, do not get carried away and make your staging too fussy. Never forget it is the setting for the plant material and should never detract from that. Suitable fabrics for your coverings are polyester or cotton sheeting, nylon jersey, casement, muslin and sparva rayon for the tabling, whilst hessian is practical for the individual low bases and the plant stall. Felt and display drape are available in a wide range of colours and although they can be difficult to clean and are easily torn in storage, both have their uses.

Choose a colour which does not detract from the flowers and which can be used over and over again. If buying in quantity, explore the possibility of dealing direct with wholesalers, otherwise markets are a good source of supply. Fabric is expensive but with care can last for years. It should be stored rolled on a cardboard tube, obtainable from the drapery department of your local store, and then covered in plastic sheeting having first of all made quite sure it is dry and clean.

The simplest covering for tables, which are staged against a wall so that only three sides are seen, is to cover the top and sides all in one. Measure the length of tabling and then add the amount required from top of table to the floor for each end. Using a 72 in. (182 cm.) wide material, lay this over the tabling leaving a clearance from the ground of 1 in. (2.5 cm.) all the way along. Hold out the side edge at the front by the bottom back corner and then fold towards the back, dropping the surplus material down between the fold and the table. Pin the fold to the table at the top with drawing pins, hiding them under the material. Double-sided adhesive tape will be required if the table tops are Formica or similar material.

Skirting the tables

If you have the minimum amount of material at your disposal and need the most economical way of skirting your tabling, it is simplest just to put the material round the tabling taut and drawing-pin it to the table or use double-sided adhesive tape.

A more attractive way which uses very little more material is to have an inverted pleat at the corners. If your tables are against a wall, start about 8 in. (20 cm.) in on the back edge, attach your material taut along the side edge until the front corner is reached. Pin it at the corner and then double back at least 4 in. (10 cm.) but preferably 6 in. (15 cm.), and pin firmly. Come back again taking the material round the corner 4 in. (10 cm.), and then underlap the same amount, pinning firmly. Continue until the next corner is reached and repeat accordingly. If your tables are double-banked, either start your material at a back corner or where the tables meet, preferably away from the main entrance in case the join is visible, as you do not want this to be the first thing visitors see.

Pleating

An alternative skirting is pleating all the way round, but this needs at least twice as much material and takes longer to put on. If both time and money are short, it could be used on one table only to stage a special class, or perhaps on the table on which the cups and trophies are displayed. It can only be used on wooden tables which will take drawing pins as it cannot be secured successfully with adhesive tape. To ensure the pleats are even you need a template. Cut a piece of very strong card 9 in. wide and 3 in. deep (22 cm. x 7.6 cm.). Mark a line 3 in. (7.6 cm.) from the left side. If the fabric is the correct width for the height of the table top from the floor use self-coloured pins, to attach it to the side of the table. If, however, the fabric is too wide, it must be folded over the top and pinned to the top as well as to the sides of the table to ensure that the pleats hang well. It is not advisable to use thick fabric such as nylon jersey because it forms a bump under the top covering if it is pinned on to the table top.

Begin at the right side of tabling as you are facing it. Put a drawing pin through the top right corner of fabric and table, lay the template on top, then fold the fabric over the left edge up to the line. Remove the card and pin the pleat. Now place the right edge of the template to the right hand of the newly formed pleat and fold on the line as before. This allows a 6 in. (15 cm.) space between right edge of each pleat, giving you evenly spaced knife pleats.

Knife pleats may be formed without any space between them allowing three times the length of fabric for the tabling. The template should be 6 in. x 3 in. (15 cm. x 7.6 cm.) with a line marked in the centre. Proceed as for evenly spaced knife pleats, thus the right hand edge of one pleat will lie on the top of the material and against the left hand edge of the previous pleat which will be underneath the fabric.

Box pleats need fabric which measures three times the length of the tabling. Follow the method described in figure 1. Only fine fabric, such as muslin or casement should be used for this type of skirting. Both of these 'take' the pleats well, especially if you pull the material slightly at the bottom following the fold of the pleat, and run your (clean) fingers up and down two or three times to 'set' the pleats. Care

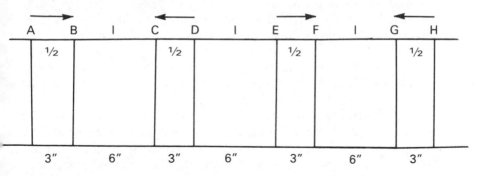

Figure 1 **To make touching box pleats**
Allow three times the measurement in material.
Fold A on B to centre of BC.
Fold D on C to centre of BC.
Fold E on F to centre of FG.
Fold H on G to centre of FG.

should be taken to choose appropriate pleating for each class. For example a class calling for the use of delicate type of plant material, miniatures or petites, would be more suited to this kind of pleating than a *pot-et-fleur* or landscape.

Gathers are yet another method of covering your tabling. Though slightly more expensive they are quick and easy to do by using Rufflette curtain tape which can be sewn round the top of the skirting and pulled to the correct measurement. This does make the skirting very versatile as it enables you to use it for varying lengths of tabling. The longer the tabling, the fewer the gathers; the shorter the tables, the greater the number of gathers. Another advantage of gathered skirting is that it can be stored on a roll by simply untieing the string and pulling out the gathers. It is also very easy to launder. Its disadvantage is that it must be attached with drawing pins to the table beneath.

Table tops

Having skirted your tables, you need to cover the tops. If all your money has been spent on skirts which will be seen much more than the table top covering and which will need to withstand people's feet kicking into them, then a cheap covering is paper. The end of a print roll may be obtained from your local newspaper offices for a few pennies. It is too short to be of use to them, but is ideal for covering tables. Lining paper obtained from wallpaper shops makes equally good table top covering, but never be tempted to use paper as a skirt on any table, however small, for it can so easily tear during the show and completely ruin the appearance of that particular class, if not the whole show.

Fabric is ideal for covering your table tops. It can either match the skirt or be of a different cloth or colour. Beware, however of using a strongly contrasting colour. You are setting the stage, and must not detract from the main item which is the exhibit which is to be placed on your staging.

A length of fabric can be layed on the table top just overlapping the top of the skirting by no more than 3 in. (7.5 cm.) thus covering up the pins or tape used for fixing the skirt. Plastic sheet can then be put on top of this to protect it against spilled water.

If you are staging a class that has any relevance to weddings or christenings, or perhaps a miniature or petite class, an alternative finish can be made with muslin or fine nylon, tied at equal intervals with bows so that a scallop is formed between each pair of bows. A band of fabric at least 12 in. (30 cm.) deep is attached to the edge of the table with double-sided adhesive tape and tied at regular intervals with ribbon, made into bows and pinned.

The same effect can be achieved by using the table top covering, allowing it to fall 12 in. (30 cm.) over the front edge, looping the surplus at intervals again with narrow ribbon or cord (figure 2). Attach a 2 ft (60 cm.) length of ribbon, cord or even thick knitting wool by means of a drawing pin under the cloth, giving you two equal ends. Bring these ends up from underneath, gathering the 12 in. (30 cm.) of cloth. Insert another drawing pin to the side of the table on top of the material, anchoring the ribbon, cord or wool firmly, and finish with a bow.

Pelmets

A pelmet used with any form of skirting can give a neat finish. This can be cut from non-fraying material and is one of the instances where it would be an advantage to use felt or display drape. A harmonizing colour rather than too strong a contrast is advisable.

The edge may be scalloped or fashioned as a chevron, and, again you need a template, cut from strong card to the pattern. The pelmet should be 5 to 6 in. (12.7 to 15 cm.) deep at the deepest point, and attached to the top of the skirting with double-sided adhesive tape.

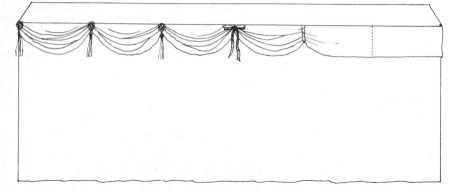

Figure 2   Making a table covering
Material for covering table top hanging 12 in. (30 cm) over front edge.
Gather evenly all along using ribbon or cord attached to the underside,
bringing it up and over to the top, fastening it with a drawing pin and
finishing off with a bow of ribbon or tassle. The table is already skirted.

A box-pleated pelmet is easily made, and if likely to be used on
more than one occasion could be pleated and sewn along the top,
before being attached to the skirting with double-sided adhesive tape
or Velcro.

Backgrounds
Unless all your class are intended to be viewed from all angles some
backgrounds will be needed. Certainly classes staged against a wall
on which there are fire-fighting appliances, light brackets or
windows will need them to give each competitor similar staging
conditions. You cannot have a competitor staging against part
window, part wall as background, or against a wall supporting a light
bracket which looks as if it is balancing on the top of her highest piece
of plant material.

Niches
Backgrounds made from cardboard niches may be obtained in
widths of 2 ft, 2 ft 6 in. and 3 ft (60, 75 and 91 cm.) with heights of
either 3 ft or 3 ft 6 in. (91 or 99 cm.). The sides, which are usually 8
to 9 in. (20-22 cm.) in this type of backing, divide the entries into
individual alcoves. Niches can be stored flat and can be kept in
spotless condition by occasionally painting with emulsion paint.
They can be held together with small bulldog clips top and bottom,
painted the same colour as they are. Painting the clips is not the time-

consuming task it sounds. The quickest way is to clip them in a row down the side of an old niche or cardboard box, and then go up and down with your paint brush. They are far less obtrusive than paper clips which are inclined to pop off at the wrong moment. If niches are to be used on double tabling (two classes back to back) ensure that niches of the same height are used in both classes.

Fabric

Backgrounds can also be made of fabric attached to dowel rods or best quality electric conduit. Do not buy the cheapest quality conduit because it will bend under the weight of the material. Sink a 6 ft (1.8 m.) length of dowel or electric conduit into large coffee tins, fruit juice cans or flower pots, painted the same colour as the skirting and filled with stones and cement. If these are twisted round gently whilst the cement is setting it will enable the poles to be removed for easier storage. Screw a cuphook to the top of each dowel on which to rest your top bar, also made of dowel, or use the corners for the conduit (figure 3). Place this framework at intervals behind the tables or between them if it is to be used as background for two classes staged back to back. If the rods used at the ends of the tabling are likely to be seen, they should be painted or bandaged with strips of staging material.

Fabric such as nylon jersey, muslin, casement, polyester or cotton sheeting can be hung across the top bar and slightly and evenly gathered to fall both sides of it for staging back-to-back classes. A class staged against a wall can have the fabric pinned or Sellotaped to the top bar. There is no necessity for the fabric to be floor-length, but it should hang at least 6 in. (15 cm.) below the table top.

The fabric used for backgrounds should not be too flimsy as the sunlight or artificial light will shine through it. If it is used for staging classes back to back it is distracting as shadows from the exhibit behind can be seen. If there is any likelihood of the light shining through, the fabric can be slightly gathered. Too many gathers make a fussy background which is not suitable for all classes.

The spaces in which the exhibits are to be staged must be marked. If the table covering is paper, a line can easily be drawn with a felt-tip pen. When fabric is used narrow tape or cord may be held in position with dressmaking pins or drawing pins. The tables should be measured at the back and front before the line is drawn or the tape is attached. A piece of square dowel 3 ft (90 cm.) long marked with 2 ft and 2 ft 6 in. (60 and 75 cm.) lengths is a great help for this job.

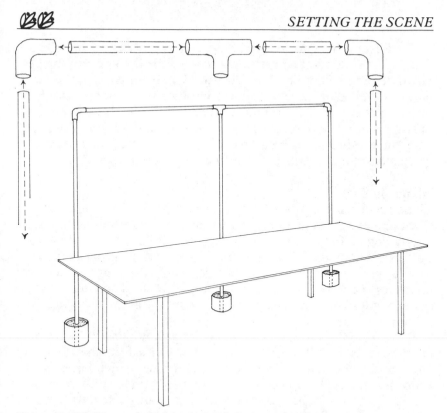

Figure 3   Backing using electric conduit
Six-foot lengths of conduit are sunk into empty coffee tins **which have**
been filled with cement. The uprights are joined to the cross-**bar at the top**
by means of elbow and T-junctions.

Hanging classes
It can be difficult to accommodate the entries which require hanging,
and stage them all at the correct height, at the same time making the
class look attractive.

   Care should always be taken to ensure that no entry is staged lower
than table height. So, it is best to have your staging, possibly peg-
board which is very suitable, standing firmly on the top of the table.
A simple method of securing this firmly to the table is by attaching a
wooden batten, 2 in. x 1 in. (5 x 2.5 cm.) either side of the peg-board
at that back to the required height. At the base of the battens screw
an angle bracket on to the inside, with the free end pointing towards
the centre of the back of the peg-board. Secure these two free ends to
the table with a 'C' clamp, obtainable from your husband's tool box
or from your local ironmonger.

Block feet can be made by using two pieces of wood 5 in. x 3 in. x 2 in. (12.7 x 7.6 x 5 cm.), cutting a channel the thickness of the peg-board centrally along the 5 in. length. The front edge of the block may be bevelled to prevent it appearing clumsy. These feet should be painted either to match the table covering or the peg-board. The peg-board is simply slotted into these, and will hold all but very heavy hanging exhibits. The peg-board may be painted or covered in wallpaper or in the same fabric as the rest of the staging.

Island sites

These are usually 2 ft 6 in. or 3 ft (75 cm. or 91 cm.) in diameter. Circular bases are more popular than square ones, although they may be any shape. They are raised 8 or 9 in. (20 or 22 cm.) from the floor by various methods. Whichever method is used, these bases must be well supported so that any part is able to take the weight of a heavy accessory such as a garden cherub or bird bath. The base must be quite steady while the arrangers are standing on it to arrange the exhibit.

One method of raising a base from the ground is with four pieces of 18 x 8 x ½ in. (45 x 20 x 1 cm.) wood formed into a square and glued to the underside of your 3 ft (90 cm. base) which has been cut from shuttering ply or chipboard. The disadvantage of this method is that the base will be bulky to store and transport, but it will be very, very firm. Shuttering ply has been suggested as it is cheaper and lighter in weight than chipboard and is therefore easier to carry and move.

An alternative method is to use two pieces of shuttering ply or chipboard 12 in. (30 cm.) shorter than the diameter of circle x 8 in. (20 cm.). Cut a slot in the centre of each piece 4 in. (10 cm.) long x the thickness of the chipboard. Slot one into the other, then lay the top across it. Before you put the top in place, cover it in fabric which has been cut 2 in. (5 cm.) larger all round and staple it to the underside of the top pulling the fabric tight as you staple to prevent it puckering. A collar of card should be cut to the correct depth, covered in matching material and attached with double-sided adhesive tape to the rim of the top. Do not be tempted to use fabric on the sides without the card lining as a sloppy rather than a tailored effect will result.

A loose cloth may also be used as an alternative covering. This should be cut to fall almost to the floor so its size should be equivalent to the diameter of the circle plus twice the height of the stand. Nylon jersey is particularly useful for this as it falls gracefully without having to be arranged and will not fray. If you do use a fabric which frays then you will need to hem it.

Carpet roll tubes can also be used to make bases. They need to be cut to the required height and four or five glued to the underside of the top. The top should be glued rather than just being placed on them, otherwise they are inclined to slip.

Pot-et-fleur

This class may be staged on individual stands made from a piece of carpet roll cut to the required height and glued to two or three circular or square boards of differing diameters forming a plinth. A further board can be attached to the top forming the platform for the container. The entire construction is then painted with flat grey paint or emulsion to which some coarse sand has been added. If they are first given a coat of size, the paint will not soak into the roll or bases. These stands may be weighted giving extra stability by inserting sand as ballast before fixing the top platform, or, for easier storage, using an empty tin filled with sand or cement at the bottom, placing the roll over it (figure 4).

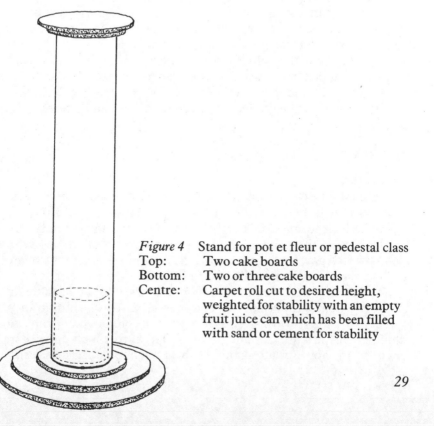

Figure 4   Stand for pot et fleur or pedestal class
Top: Two cake boards
Bottom: Two or three cake boards
Centre: Carpet roll cut to desired height, weighted for stability with an empty fruit juice can which has been filled with sand or cement for stability

Pedestals

The stands as described for *pot-et-fleur* may be cut slightly taller and used for pedestals. They can be covered in marbled Fablon rather than with paint and sand.

When staging a pedestal class allow a minimum of 4 ft (1.2 m.) space in front of each exhibit to enable it to be judged from the correct position.

Miniatures

Cake board holders (as used between tiers of a wedding cake) make ideal individual pedestals or stands for miniatures. It is advisable to select circular ones rather than the square variety which are inclined to look heavier.

Sales tables

Tables which are being used for cakes, plants and flower arranging accessories will all need covers. These should be in the same staging material as used elsewhere to tie in with the overall colour scheme. If your staging material is thin and delicate you may wish to use hessian in a similar or toning colour for the plant stall.

The importance of display on these tables cannot be stressed too strongly. Your aim is to sell, therefore you must attract the visiting public to these tables. Articles staged at different heights gives you more overall table room and look more attractive. If boxes covered in fabric or wallpaper are used in the display, items such as pressed flower pictures and book marks may be propped against them. Covered boxes can be graded in size so that they can be stored inside each other.

PLACING THE NOTICES

Class titles

These should be clear, easy to read and placed above people's heads. They may be fastened to the wall above the class with Blutac, or if this is neither permissible nor possible, a special stand can be made for them using the same method of sinking a 6 ft (1.8 m.) dowel rod into a painted pot, tin or flower pot, the rod being painted or covered, and the class title firmly attached to the top.

The lettering must be as professional as possible, undertaken by a member who has experience in commercial display printing, or you could experiment with Letraset which is obtainable from most stationers in various sizes and colours. The card which you use may be cut to any appropriate shape, such as a bell for a Christmas show, a large leaf, or a daisy with the lettering in the centre. The possibilities are endless.

Competitors' class cards

These should be approximately 5 x 4 in. (12 x 10 cm.) and printed on both sides. Smaller ones, half this size may be used for miniature or petite classes. On the front should be the name of the society or club, the title of the show, a space for award stickers, the title of the class and the competitor's name and address.

The reverse side, which must be on display whilst judging is taking place, will require only the class number and competitor's number. These cards with the front on display should be placed in the space where the competitors are to stage their entries, indicating their position when they arrive. The competition secretary must ensure that the reverse sides of the cards are showing before judging starts, turning them to the front only when all judging is complete.

Exhibition arrangement

A centre piece placed in the main hall to represent the whole show, or arranged in the entrance hall to welcome visitors, could be undertaken by one or more club members who no longer wish to compete. They appreciate being invited to be part of the show, and the public is glad of the opportunity to see their work.

3. Compiling the Schedule

This is certainly a responsibility, but what an exciting one. The world is your oyster. There is so much from which to choose for your theme. Surely there is not a subject that could not be portrayed in flowers. While this is true, there are many subjects which can more easily be associated with flowers than others and from which countless imaginative class titles can be taken. Inspiration may come from plays, poems, books, music, the arts, other hobbies, crafts and pastimes, pages of history, the seasons, the countryside, the sea – the list is endless, inspiring and challenging. Make your schedule just as inspiring and challenging.

CHOOSING A THEME

First choose your theme. Then select your overall title and class titles which must relate to each other and carry out your theme. The title and your schedule make all the difference to your show; its success or failure depends on the quality of the schedule. If it is inspiring the entries will flood in; if it is interesting it will attract the public as well as the press.

The theme should make people feel compelled to enter, eager to be part of this splendid show. How often have we heard the excuse, 'The schedule does not inspire me', and how often is this true? Competitors may be enthusiastic but it is your schedule which should encourage them to create an exhibit with that little extra distinction which will result in a sparkling show. Poor schedules will not produce interesting shows.

The competition secretary should not expect, or be expected to produce a first-class schedule on her own. She may have the idea for a theme and a title, but a small group of people, or sub-committee are more likely to produce a better schedule than a competition secretary working on her own. She may sow seeds, and ideas will then germinate, be discussed and the best ones adopted.

The wording, which should be concise, must at the same time leave no doubt in the minds of either the competitors or the judge as to what is required. It is so easy to have confusing wording in the classes. *You* know what you want, but will the wording produce the

I 'Spectrum', staged by Rita Hill and Joyce Busby.

The primary colours are depicted by spray carnations, gerberas and delphiniums and the arrangements are linked by the use of painted cane. Bases of the same colours form pools of light.

II 'Kubla Khan', staged by Kevin Gunnell.

The colouring of the plant material used in this exhibit gives the feeling of opulence, in this instance oriental opulence. Here is Kubla Khan perhaps in Court Dress for a ceremonial occasion, hence the dagger, jewels and drape indicative of a person of great presence. The blue glass ornament links the base and blue delphiniums, and the scale of the flowers in relation to the accessories is good.

type of exhibit you envisage, or will it be misunderstood which could lead to disqualification? This is where the judge can help you by vetting the schedule before you have it printed or duplicated, so send her a draft copy at this stage.

BASIC CONSIDERATIONS

When planning your schedule thought should be given to the following points.

1 The time of the year and availability of plant material. For example, it would be preferable to include a foliage class in the autumn when foliage is more plentiful, more colourful and easier to condition, than in the spring when it is new and inclined to wilt far more quickly however well it has been conditioned. By contrast an 'all green' class would be better in the summer when there is more choice of flowers such as zinnia, gladioli, nicotiana and roses as well as foliage for the exhibitors to use.

2 Including a number of different styles to cater for all competitors and to give a more interesting look to the show. These might, for example, be traditional; period; abstract; interpretative; landscape; pot et fleur; miniature or petite; pedestal; dinner or buffet table; swags, plaques, picture or collages; modern.

3 Specifying classes requiring different types of plant material, for example, sophisticated, miniature, woodland, natural plant material, fresh plant material, and dried and glycerined.

In selecting titles for classes, care should be exercised with the choice of words, avoiding 'of', for example, 'of fruit and vegetables', which can be restricting and may even lead to disqualification. It is better to use instead 'to predominate' or 'featuring', for example 'featuring fresh foliage' or 'fresh plant material to predominate' which mean that your fresh plant material must be more visually dominant than the rest of the exhibit.

4 Including a simple class for beginners to encourage them and choosing a title which will give them guidance. It is often seeing a simple exhibit staged by a beginner that encourages visitors to the show to join the club. They realize there is something they could do.

5 Choose interpretative classes requiring research which will stretch the imagination and skill of the more experienced competitor.

6 Including classes which need varied types of staging and not merely rows of tabling.

7 Including classes in which backgrounds, accessories and painted plant material are *not* allowed.

8 The number of classes which can be staged well in the space available, the number of entries to be staged in each class, and the amount of money available for prizes, staging and other items.

PREPARING THE DRAFT

Your schedule should contain all the information the competitors are likely to need leaving them in no doubt as to what they may or may not do. It will also prevent you from having to answer numerous queries.

For the benefit of the competitors include the following information:

Eligibility (whether she is able to enter every class or whether specific qualifications are required for certain classes)

Entry fee and to whom it should be sent

Closing date for entries

Cancellation restrictions

Times of staging and dismantling

Size of display area (width, depth and height)

Colour and height of backing and table tops

If the exhibit is to be staged against a backing or whether it will be viewed from all sides

If the position for the exhibit is allocated by the committee

If and when competitors' backgrounds are allowed

If drapes and backgrounds may be attached to the staging

If exhibits must be arranged on the premises or whether they may be brought ready assembled, for example; a miniature, swag or picture

Liability for loss, damage and personal injury

Details of awards and trophies, also time of prizegiving

Times of judging and name/s of judge/s

Whether the show is being judged according to any particular set of rules, for example according to the NAFAS *Handbook of Schedule Definitions*

Whether the judges' decision is final

That competitors must leave the hall during judging

Any instructions regarding photography, whether it is allowed, and if so, when

The competition secretary's name, address and telephone number

The telephone number of the venue on show day as this enables competitors to contact the competiton secretary at the show venue in cases of emergency.

For the benefit of the public include the following details:
Full name of the club, society or organization
Venue date and times of opening
Show Title and admission fee
Car parking facilities
Charity donation (if any)
Opener or personality attending
Special attractions
Refreshments
Information about the club, society or organization
For the benefit of the judge: allow her to perform her very responsible job without the fear of time running out because the public are waiting to get in. Allowing insufficient time is unfair to the judge, the competitors and the show committee.

A draft schedule should always be sent to the judge before being printed or duplicated so that she can approve the wording. This helps to avoid problems and possible disqualifications which can arise from ambiguous phrasing in the schedule.

Word sequence of instructions should be consistent. For example, if you start with the type of plant material allowed, followed by the size of space and end with any other instructions, such as no accessories, in one class, then do not in the following class begin with the size of space, followed by what you cannot use and finish with the type of plant material. Keep your instructions, which should be brief, in the same order throughout.

When you have finished your draft, visualize the effect the schedule will have on the show when it is staged. Ask yourself whether it will encourage different styles of exhibits; whether it will ensure a variety of plant material; if it will result in entries of beauty and novelty; and if it will produce the best show ever . . . . until the next time.

A SAMPLE SCHEDULE

This is a suggested schedule for a large club show entitled 'A Summer Season of Theatre and Flowers' to be held in early July. All measurement are given in feet and inches only, a metric conversion table being found at the end of the book.

Class 1 – Gala night
A pedestal exhibit
Staged on a raised base 4 ft 6 in. square, six inches from floor, and

against a pale grey background 7 ft high (from top of base). Base covered and skirted in pale grey.

Class 2 – Overture (Beginners)
An exhibit
Space 2 ft 6in. wide x 3 ft high
This class open only to members who have not previously entered a competitive show.

Class 3 – Variety bill (Inter-club)
A group exhibit
Staged on round island base 4 ft in diameter, 1 ft from floor, covered and skirted in apricot-coloured felt. Other base coverings may be used but must not extend over edge
To be viewed all round
Maximum of three members.

Class 4 – Drama
'An abstract exhibit
Space 2 ft 6 in. wide x 3 ft 6 in. high (maximum)
Own backgrounds to be provided.

Class 5 – Poetry and Prose (Novice)
An exhibit depicting a quotation of own choice
Space 2 ft 6 in. wide x 3 ft high
Quotation and name of author to be included
This class open only to members who have not won an award in a competitive show.

Class 6 – Puppet show
A petite exhibit
Staged on a round tiered table covered and skirted in pale apricot fabric. Two levels 14 in. apart.
Viewed from front only.

Class 7 – Wardrobe mistress
An exhibit incorporating at least two fabrics
Space 3 ft wide x 3 ft 6 in. high

Class 8 – The green room
An exhibit
Fresh plant material excluding flowers

Space 2 ft 6 in. wide x 3 ft. high

Class 9 – Lighting design
A modern or abstract exhibit
Space 2 ft 6 in. wide x 3 ft 6 in. high

Class 10 – On with the show (advanced)
An exhibit depicting any play (not musical) that has appeared in the
    West End of London. Staged on low tabling 2 ft from floor. Space
    3 ft wide x 2 ft deep x 4ft high
Staging and background covered in apricot-coloured fabric
This class open only to qualified demonstrators, judges and teachers
Name of play to be displayed.

Staging instructions
Unless otherwise stated all classes staged on tabling approximately
    2 ft 9 in. high x 2 ft 3 in. deep
Coverings and backgrounds in pale grey
All measurements are approximate
All backgrounds, drapes, etc. must be supported and not attached to
    staging
No artificial material allowed in any class.

COMMENTS ON THE SCHEDULE

The class for beginners – Class 2 entitled 'Overture', provides just a little something extra to stimulate the imagination, although in this case just a piece of sheet music would be sufficient. If any beginner produces more, she should be given great credit. This will help beginners to learn from the start the importance of relating plant material with other objects. All competition work involves more than 'doing flowers nicely', and if this is realized from the start a great deal more satisfaction is gained from show work.

    The class for novices – Class 5 with the title 'Poetry and Prose' may appear a little advanced for a novice class but it allows competitors to choose a quotation which is as easy or difficult as they wish.

    Class 8 entitled 'The green room' which requires 'fresh plant material excluding flowers' is a different way of describing a foliage class. But it allows more scope for the inclusion of seedheads, buds, grasses, cones, and fruit.

4. Entering the Show

Why do we enter shows? To improve the standard of our work. For the fun, the pure enjoyment and experience, and not with the idea of winning a prize. No one wins every time and a great deal of satisfaction is to be gained from just knowing that your exhibit was impeccably staged; that you have tackled something different; that you have discovered something you did not know about the subject of your class title thereby increasing your general knowledge; and that you have widened your staging experience gaining confidence for next time. At the same time you have given pleasure to the public and supported the committee organizing the show.

Competing is an incentive to do our best, exciting but a little frightening when we enter for the first time. If you are a member of a local flower club it is almost certain they will hold competitions at their monthly meetings. This is the ideal place to commence your 'showing career'. Here you will have your work criticized. Do not be afraid of what will be said about your exhibit, you can learn so much from listening to the constructive advice given. It is only by having our work commented upon that we learn to improve. Listen to what the judge has to say about all the entries; learn by other people's mistakes as well as your own; and compare your work with that of the other competitors. Visit any of the local shows which include a flower arranging section. Study the schedule, paying special attention to how it has been interpreted. Read the judge's comment cards which will explain to the competitor and visiting public the reason why, perhaps through poor interpretation or non-adherance to the schedule, the entry has failed to win an award although, in some cases it may be a better arrangement than the winner. Then take the plunge. I am certain you will never regret it.

ENTRY PROCEDURE

Where to begin? Obtain the schedule for the show. If you are not a member of the club or association which is staging the show, and there is no name and address on the poster advertising the event, enquire at the hall where it is being held and you will be given a name to contact. Read the schedule carefully, from cover to cover. Familiarize yourself with any rules and requirements, and, if the show is being judged in accordance with the NAFAS *Handbook of Schedule Definitions*, it is important that you understand these as well, and equally as important to ensure you are in possession of the latest edition because they do alter slightly from time to time.

Only then will you fully understand the schedule and appreciate exactly what you are being called upon to do and to use. If however, the show is not being judged in accordance with the NAFAS *Handbook of Schedule Definitions*, you may find the classes call for 'an arrangement of . . .', whereas a show judged by the seventh edition of the NAFAS *Handbook* would state 'an exhibit' in place of the words 'arrangement' or 'design'. 'An exhibit' is plant material, with or without accessories, contained within the space specified in the show schedule. Bases, drapes, backgrounds and title cards may also be included in an exhibit unless otherwise stated.

If there is anything which perplexes you, contact the show secretary, whose address and telephone number will be found on the schedule. She helped compile the schedule and will almost certainly have the answer to your problem. Pick out one or preferably two classes which appeal to you, making sure you are eligible to enter them. Some classes are limited to, for example, beginners or advanced members, club members only, or are inter-club classes.

SELECTING THE CLASSES

Included in some schedules is a class for competitors who have never won a prize in a show before. This is an ideal class in which to start. Do not enter too many classes the first time. Two are ideal and better than just one. With one you may find you are too engrossed with that single exhibit, whereas with two your attention is divided. When you have finished staging your second exhibit you can go back to your first one with fresh eyes.

Fill in your entry form and send it together with the entry fee to the competition secretary, making sure it reaches her well on time. It is encouraging for the committee to know that the entries are coming in and the show is being well supported. It also indicates which classes are proving popular, and whether any particular class is likely to be over-subscribed, or perhaps not quite filled, allowing time for adjustments to be made to the staging. Some shows limit the number of entries in each class, so it is best to send in your form early.

PLANNING YOUR EXHIBIT

Look up each word of the title of your chosen class/es in a dictionary even if you think you know the meaning of every word used, and write down everything that comes to mind. The more experienced competitor will dismiss the obvious interpretations and pursue the idea which is not quite so evident.

Never be tempted to copy from books. Points are awarded for originality, and the judge may have seen the picture, or even judged the original if it is a photograph of an entry at a previous show. Judges do travel far afield and have most retentive memories.

Read the wording which follows the title carefully. This will give you the size of the space allowed, the type of staging and the colour of your backing and base or table top. Also read the instructions as to the type of plant material which you may use, such as 'foliage only', whether accessories are allowed, and, in a Christmas show, in which classes, if any, you are allowed to use paint and glitter.

When deciding on your plant material do not be misled into thinking you must use expensive flowers. It is the well chosen, well conditioned, most suitable plant material for the class which will win points, not the most extravagant one.

A well written schedule will contain no ambiguous wording but will say in the least number of words exactly what you may or may not do and use. If the wording just calls for 'an exhibit' and you are being judged in accordance with the NAFAS *Handbook of Schedule Definitions*, then you may use more than one placement, any type of plant material, even artificially coloured, with base, drape or background and accessories. But always check the rules and regulations by which the show is being judged. Miniature and table classes are slightly different, therefore when making your selection and when staging either of these classes the following points should be remembered.

MINIATURES

These should not exceed 4 in. (10 cm.) in height, width or depth, and should be an exact replica of a large arrangement following the same principles of design so that when magnified ten times the whole would be in proportion.

Containers

Thimbles, tops of perfume or cosmetic bottles, small shells and ornaments are amongst some of the items which make useful containers. If you experience any difficulty in finding a suitable pedestal-type container in which to stage your miniature, it is very simple to make your own (figure 5). You require the nozzle from two empty washing-up liquid containers, a length of size nine knitting needle 1 in. (2.5 cm.) long which will fit into the nozzles, one being used as your base, and the other reversed at the top becoming your container for your water-retaining foam. Plasticine may be inserted into the one at the base giving it a little extra weight, or it may be glued on to a flat button for stability, and then the whole 'pedestal' sprayed with paint.

Figure 5 Hand-made pedestal for miniature exhibit
Top: The top of a washing up container holding water-retaining foam
Middle: Short length of knitting needle
Bottom: (a) Top of a washing up container
          (b) Thick card base covered in fabric

Tools

Your working tools will be different. Instead of your flower scissors use a pair of nail scissors which will give a cleaner cut on the thin stems. Tweezers are invaluable for inserting the flower stems into the water-retaining foam or damp sand. Care should be exercised when using tweezers. Hold the stem as near the bottom as possible, not too tightly otherwise you will either sever the stem or it will become squashed, an air lock will form, and water will be unable to reach the top. A long darning needle is useful for making holes in the water-retaining foam before inserting the fragile stems.

Plant material

A rockery provides the largest selection of suitable plants, although it is perfectly possible to find sufficient material eslewhere in the garden amongst the herbs, and also in the hedgrows. This requires the same careful conditioning as plant material used for larger exhibits. The ends of the stems should be boiled for five seconds, and then left in tepid water. Watering your miniature after it has been arranged may be achieved by means of a dropper, and spraying, which is invaluable, can be done with a fine scent spray.

Transporting your exhibit

Miniatures need time and patience, and for this reason you are sometimes permitted to enter a miniature which has been arranged at home. In this case great care must be taken when transporting it to the show because it can be damaged so easily. It is always advisable to take a few 'spares' with you, especially outline plant material. The finished exhibit should be placed upright in a box or empty food carton with crumpled tissue or kitchen paper packed round the container to keep it from moving. If your exhibit has been arranged in a flat container, for the journey you can anchor its base with oasis fix to a heavy, flat piece of wood sufficiently large not to topple over. In very warm weather it may be advantageous to leave your exhibit in the refrigerator overnight. Thoroughly spray the completed exhibit before placing it in a box with a lid, or cover the top of the box with a plastic bag fastened securely by an elastic band.

Bases

Bases are as useful to a miniature as they are to a larger exhibit, but they must be in proportion. Small pieces of slate, stone, wood or mirror may be used, or a base can be made from card covered in Fablon to resemble marble, or in fabric. To cover a card base, cut a piece of fabric to shape, allowing an extra ½ in. (1 cm.) for turn-in, which should be notched at intervals. Spread glue round the edge of the card on the underside; lay the right side of the card to the wrong side of the fabric; fold the turn-in over on to the underside, overlapping the notches to take up surplus fabric, keeping it pulled tightly to avoid puckers, but not so tightly that it buckles the card. Cut another piece of fabric slightly smaller than the base and glue to the underside. If the fabric is inclined to fray, wallpaper or Fablon may be used to neaten the underside. Narrow braid or cord may be glued round the edge as a finish.

TABLE CLASSES

It could be lack of staging space which precludes many schedules from including a table class. This is unfortunate because it adds variety to the staging and also calls for a different style. Table classes are particularly popular with members of the public, possibly because they give them ideas for their own homes.

Accessories

When planning your entry ascertain from the schedule whether it is for a formal or informal lunch or dinner party (a seated table) or for a buffet; whether the table covering is provided or you are expected to provide your own. If the latter, it must be spotlessly clean and without a crease. The colour and texture of the cloth must tone with the china, accessories and plant material, and they should all be an appropriate choice for the occasion in mind.

For example, an 'al fresco' lunch calls for a coarse linen cloth in a plain colour rather than gingham, which, although the correct material for the class title, would be too fussy for your plant material. Pottery would be a better choice than bone china, with your plant material arranged in a basket or pottery container, using zinnias, dahlias, geraniums or something similar rather than freesia or spray carnations in a pale colour. By contrast, a celebration dinner party calls for a more delicate table covering of fine linen or lace, bone china and a traditional style of arrangement with roses and pale spray carnations in an elegant container.

As always, read your schedule carefully because a decorated table could have more than one exhibit, but do not be tempted to fill the table with either exhibits or accessories just because you have them. Remember the main purpose of the table is to take a meal, so leave room for the food. One exception is a table decoration in Victorian style. In the Victorian era it was 'the more the merrier': as well as a central epergne, garlands of ivy or smilax interspersed with small flowers would be arranged on the table, covering most of the space. There would also be a small posy or garland for each person seated at table.

Height of exhibits

Exhibits for seated tables should be kept low. They should be no more than 12 in. (30 cm.) high to enable guests to see and chat across the table, rather than peering round the flowers. For a buffet table candlesticks or any pedestal-type container can be used to raise the plant material above the food. Care should be taken to prevent it from dripping into the food.

But it is not always essential to use a pedestal-type container for a buffet table exhibit. You may wish to use fruit in a larger quantity and plant material in a less delicate form and colour than would look happy in a candlestick or tall container. A teenagers' party, Boxing Day lunch or a harvest supper may be just such an occasion when the exhibit would look happier on a base used as your container, so that your plant material and fruit is 'contained' on the base, whether it is a copper tray, a rush mat or a fabric-covered board. The plant material should be chosen with care. Include interesting plant material which could be a talking point, but avoid any flowers or foliage with a pungent smell, such as ruta, Choisya ternata, ribes or hyacinths as they will conflict with the food and the bouquet of the wine.

5. Choosing your Components

Once you have listed all your ideas for the class title you must decide upon your colour scheme and all the components to turn your idea into reality. Choose a container which is most suited to the style of your exhibit and the title of the class and the best mechanics to use with it. Decide whether a base and background or drape will improve the whole picture and if so, whether you have one that is correct for the exhibit or whether you need to cover or make one. Consider whether you need accessories. To help you decide which components are the most suitable for a particular class of exhibit, there follows a few points on each for guidance. First let us consider accessories.

ACCESSORIES

What are accessories? Accessories are anything other than plant material in its natural form. They may be ornaments, figurines, plates, shells, sea-fern, coral, stones, candles, fans, books, feathers etc. Take care when using animals or birds carved from wood which is plant material, because you are then using plant material in an unnatural way making them accessories. Even a bird's nest, made from plant material and untouched by human hands is an accessory because it has been fashioned into an unnatural shape, so do not use them in classes which forbid the use of accessories.

Why do we need accessories? They assist to interpret the theme. They should compliment but never predominate over the plant material, and should help to make a pleasing picture. They should be used in moderation and chosen with care, so that they are neither tawdry nor gimmicky. They should be in proportion and play a necessary part in the exhibit, and not be added as an afterthought. Never overpower your plant material with accessories just because you happen to have them. Do not for example, include fishing net, shells, seaweed, sea-fan, coral, stones, *and* driftwood in a seascape, or copper pots and pans, jelly moulds, mixing bowl, wooden spoons *and* eggs for a farmhouse kitchen. That may sound exaggerated but it does happen.

An excellent way of finding out which accessories add that certain something to your exhibit is to collect everything which you had thought of using and which relates to the class title, and add them to your exhibit. Then gradually remove them, one by one, and see if they are missed or whether it is better without them. After all you do not need to use them unless the class specifically states 'with an accessory'.

The positioning of your accessories is very important. To ensure they are well placed and form an integral part of your exhibit, arrange them first and work your plant material in afterwards. If placed in isolation or at the front of an exhibit they will appear larger than when placed near the back, and could result in being too dominant. They should be well grouped, not scattered.

If an accessory needs to be raised to give it that little extra height, or to prevent the bottom being hidden by plant material, raise it on a box or food tin. This can either be hidden by the drape, if one is being used, or can be covered in the same fabric as your base. It is impossible to match the covering of the box with the base if the latter is a wood slice, slate or tile, in which case use hessian in the appropriate colour.

Candles

When using candles, which are accessories, choose soft colours in order not to detract from the flowers. Candles may be used in candlesticks on their own, or within the arrangement, in which case the plant material must be kept well below the flame of the candle.

Do not be tempted to push the candle straight into the water-retaining foam or on to the pin holder. A much easier and more reliable method, which ensures the candle is steady and leaves more room for the plant material, is to make false legs with cocktail sticks (figure 6). Four should be plenty unless the candle is very big. Bind these round the end of the candle with florists' tape or Sellotape, leaving at least 1 in. (3 cm.) jutting out at the end of the candle.

If using more than one candle, vary the heights by cutting a small portion from the end with a warm knife, rather than by varying the length of the false legs, as these need to be concealed by your plant material and the entire length of the legs should be inserted into the water-retaining foam or pinholder for stability.

Figurines

When not used as containers figurines are accessories, and as with all accessories should relate in scale, colour and texture to the other

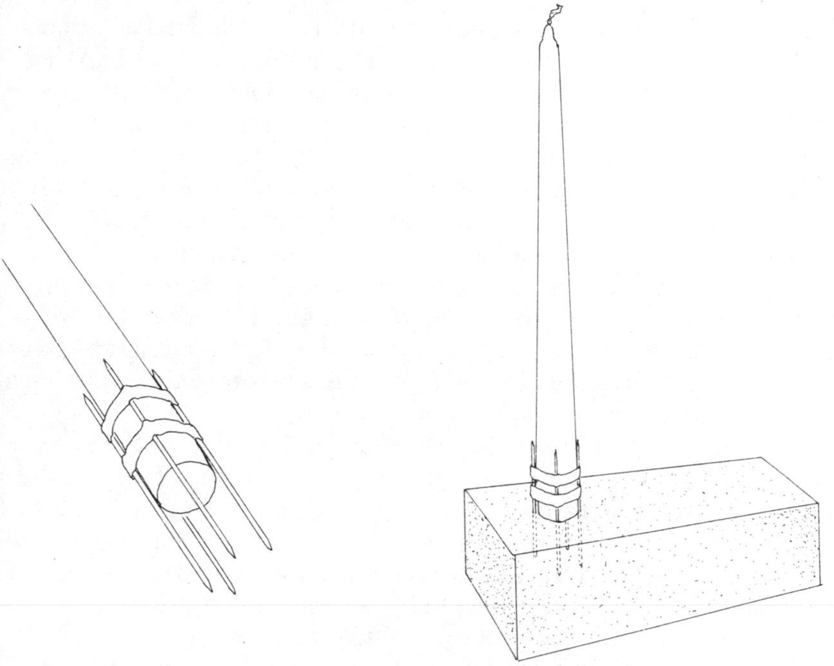

Figure 6 Securing candles
Four cocktail sticks bound round the end of a candle with florist's tape or Sellotape. The bottom half of the sticks are then inserted into the water-retaining foam. This same method may be used for supporting light driftwood.

components used in the exhibit. When using dainty figurines then use dainty flowers; if you use a sleek, modern figurine then see that your arrangement is in a similar style. If your figurine is slightly short for your exhibit, raise it as explained under accessories.

If you feel that a figurine is called for in your exhibit and you do not possess one which is suitable, you can make one using wire netting and cloth soaked in Polyfilla, or as described very clearly in a leaflet published by NAFAS and entitled 'Home Made Figurines'. This and making your own containers is another avenue well worth exploring.

CONTAINERS

The container which you may use may be seen or unseen, and made of almost anything which holds water or is adapted to hold water. It should be adequate in size but not over large for the selected plant material. It is sometimes possible to find a bargain at a jumble sale or

'Granny's Attic' market. Nothing should be overlooked as almost anything can be adapted to hold water. If cracked it can be lined with extra strong cooking foil before the water-retaining foam is inserted, or it may be sealed by melting a candle and pouring the wax into the container, turning it until the inside is well covered.

If visible, your container can and should enhance the exhibit, blending with the flowers and not vying with them for attention, so avoid using one which is highly patterned or brilliantly coloured. Brown, grey, beige, soft green or terracotta are better container colours than black or white which although neutral are very dominant. A shiny texture detracts from the plant material, but do not discard such a container. A coat of emulsion paint works wonders and it can be washed off afterwards.

Metal containers do have the advantage of keeping the water and therefore the plant material cool, helping it to last longer, and at the same time are excellent for creating atmosphere. The disadvantage is, they can be very eye-catching because they are so shiny, but this can be overcome to a certain extent, especially with brass and copper, by using flowers which are equally strong and vibrant. Pewter harmonizes well with grey foliage, blues, mauves and pinks. Pink also looks well in silver especially pink roses, sweet peas and freesias, but again care should be taken to ensure the plant material is more dominant than the container, because silver can be very distracting although not quite so powerful as brass and copper.

Containers play an extremely important part in both abstract and period exhibits. So often in abstract your ingenuity is stretched to the full, fashioning and concealing an adequate container, whilst period exhibits need containers 'of the period' or cleverly made to look 'of the period'.

The type of container chosen should compliment the flowers you are to use. For instance, if using orchids, freesias or sweet peas, then delicate china or silver would be a more suitable choice than pottery, which would be better with heavier flowers such as marigolds, zinnias and dahlias. Almost any plant material appears suitable in baskets, perhaps because baskets and basketry are natural plant material themselves.

Car spray paint is a very useful addition to your flower arranging equipment. There are many lovely colours including metallic ones. Do not, however, be surprised if, when purchasing car paint from a garage, you are regarded somewhat strangely when, on being asked which colour you want, you ask to see the range, and purchase two or three colours, all completely different from that of your car.

III Garland and Plaque of dried and glycerined plant material; shells pick up the colouring used in the memorial which the arrangement is embellishing.

IV Three arrangements complementing the window which commemorates the Royal Army Medical Corps. Staged by Richard Jeffery.

V An arrangement complementing a church vestment. The colour of the flowers which include carnations, lilies and roses picks up the colour of the embroidery. Staged by Mary Napper.

Containers take on a new lease of life when given a quick 'squirt' of car spray. Use more than one colour whilst the first is still wet, and then rub it over with shoe polish to take away the newness. An inexpensive plastic urn can be turned into an 'antique treasure' by spraying it with gold or silver paint, allowing it to dry, then spraying it quickly and lightly with matt black, which is wiped off before it has had time to dry, some remaining in the cracks and crevices of the container. A 'pewter' pot can be produced by painting a container with aluminium paint and when almost dry following the same procedure as for 'antiquing'.

As with all components, containers are taken into consideration when the exhibit is judged, therefore, do not experiment with your paints the night before the show. Practise well beforehand so that your container will be a credit to you and your exhibit.

Electric lamp stands are easily converted by means of a universal bowl which, can be screwed on to the stand after the light fittings have been removed. Whether containers are seen or unseen, delicate or heavy, ensure your mechanics are firmly fixed. Anchor your pinholders with knobs of Plasticine or Oasis – fix your water-retaining foam with foam holders and then tape, and tie your wire netting in securely. If using water-retaining foam it cannot be emphasized too strongly not to pack it into your containers too tightly – leave space for watering.

BASES

A base is the part of your exhibit on which the container stands. Nearly all exhibits look better on a base which should be treated as part of the whole exhibit. When used they are considered to be part of the container and are therefore not an accessory and should be chosen with as much care and at the same time as your container.

All types of material may be used with the exception of artificial grass. Remember that any base must be in keeping with the style and mood of the exhibit, texture being a most important factor to consider. Straw mats, bamboo, cork and hessian are good for use with basketry and pottery. Wood slices, stone and slate are appropriate for landscapes, seascapes and preserved plant material. Tiles and Perspex are suitable with modern arrangements. For traditional arrangements, marble, alabaster or boards covered in velvet or nylon-jersey fabric would all be in keeping with this style.

Fibre boards are now obtainable in a variety of shapes and sizes, and are easily covered with fabric, either glued to give you a permanent cover or for use with 'mob-caps'. For a permanent covering, the following method can be used for thick fabric such as velvet which can become bulky when gathered. Cut your fabric to the shape of your base allowing approximately 2 in. (5 cm.) extra all round. Apply a coating of glue (UHU or Copydex) round the edge only. Lay your fabric on top and insert a dressmaking pin into the fabric, choosing the straight of the material if possible. Pull it tight and insert another pin at the opposite side. Continue round, pulling the fabric tight and inserting pins every 2 in. (5 cm.). As you progress you may need to use a little more glue because it dries very quickly. When completed, turn base to underside and with a sharp pair of scissors cut of surplus fabric. Glue braid or cord round the edge thus covering all the pins. An alternative method you can use to make a permanent covering is described on page 42, but use fibre board instead of card.

Fibre boards or cake boards covered with 'mob-caps' are most useful. This way one board may have several covers in different fabrics, texture and colours which are easily removed for washing. Cut a circle or oval of fabric 3 in. (8 cm.) larger than the board. Turn and machine a ¾ in. (2 cm.) hem, leaving a small opening to insert narrow elastic. Pull the elastic fairly tight so that the fabric is pulled taut and no wrinkles or puckers appear after it is pulled over the base. Braid or cord may be pinned round rather than glued so that it can be removed. The ends of the braid or cord should have a small piece of Sellotape or a dab of nail varnish to prevent them from fraying.

If you are using a square base which you intend covering with fabric, cut the fabric the size of the board, plus the depth, plus 1 in. (2.5 cm.). Glue along the underside to the depth of 1 in. (2.5 cm.) from the edge and wrap your base in the fabric, pulling to ensure there are no wrinkles, and folding the side edges over first, then the back and front. Folded in this sequence no fold on the front is visible and there is no necessity to use braid or ribbon unless desired.

Most bases look better raised slightly, as well as being easier to pick up. Strips of polythene draught-proofing foam such as used round doors and windows make excellent cushions when the backing is peeled off and they are attached to the underside. Small plastic self-adhesive hooks, cotton reels, rubber buffers and tap washers all make excellent feet, glued or screwed to the underside and painted if they are likely to show. When using one base on top of another, space can be achieved by inserting flat tins or even table mats between the two, just raising the top one slightly which gives a more pleasing effect.

A correctly proportioned base can establish the balance as well as 'marry' the whole exhibit especially when two placements are used. An exhibit may be termed 'over-based' if the base is too big, shows too much, or its colour is too dominant. Use one that tones with the colour of your plant material, especially when you use a neutral-coloured or unseen container, such as a flat tin or dish, which will be hidden when the exhibit is complete, thus making your base your container.

BACKGROUNDS

Apart from using a base you may also need a background which should never overpower or distract from your plant material but should compliment the whole exhibit. It may be made of wood, cardboard or hardboard and should be free-standing. A simple method of achieving this is by using four brackets. Have your background cut in whatever material you have chosen, in the size and shape required. Attached two 3 in. (7.5 cm.) brackets to the back approximately 5 in. (12.5 cm.) in from the side edge, and two similar brackets in front giving you a pair of feet. These feet should be painted to match the background. Place a weight, such as a small piece of lead or a spare pinholder, on the back feet, and put your base over the feet on the front, thus making your background secure.

A more complex background-cum-base which is extremely firm but which may need the help of a handyman to construct, although it is easier to put together then would appear, is shown overleaf (figure 7).

A variety of textures may be achieved by covering the board with any type of fabric – cork, Fablon, wallpaper, hessian or even sandpaper and painting over it, or it may simply be painted without first covering it. If this is the method you choose, it is helpful to brush it over with cold-water size to prevent the paint soaking into the board, before applying any paint. The colour should be subtle and subdued. You should avoid strong colours which would be too dominant, portraying an idea rather than an exact resemblance to buildings such as castles, or churches. They may be trimmed with mouldings from your local DIY shop. These should be glued on and then painted in the same colour as the background rather than picked out in a contrasting colour, so that they create the required atmosphere without becoming too dominant. DIY shops are a source of inspiration for bases, backgrounds and staging mechanics generally.

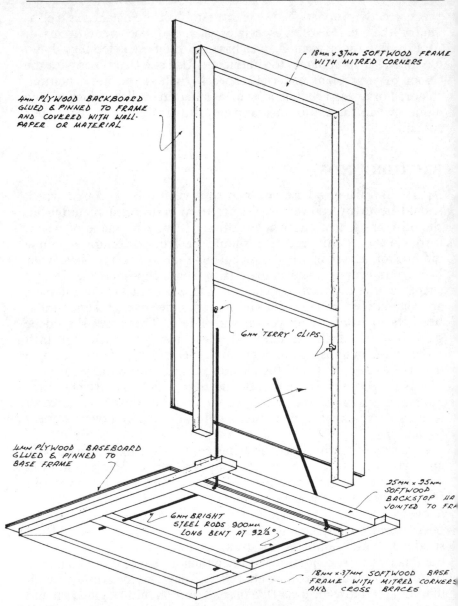

18mm x 37mm SOFTWOOD FRAME WITH MITRED CORNERS

4mm PLYWOOD BACKBOARD GLUED & PINNED TO FRAME AND COVERED WITH WALL-PAPER OR MATERIAL

6mm 'TERRY' CLIPS.

4mm PLYWOOD BASEBOARD GLUED & PINNED TO BASE FRAME

6mm BRIGHT STEEL RODS 900mm LONG BENT AT 92½°

25mm x 25mm SOFTWOOD BACKSTOP HA... JOINTED TO FRA...

18mm x 37mm SOFTWOOD BASE FRAME WITH MITRED CORNERS AND CROSS BRACES

REVERSE OF BACKBOARD ASSEMBLY VIEWED FROM THE UNDERSIDE

Figure 7 Constructing a backboard24 in. wide x 31 in. high
(610 x 787 mm.)

1   Buy a piece of 4 mm. plywood 48 in. x 24 in. (1220 x 610 mm.) and cut
    into two pieces, 30 in. x 24 in. (457 x 610 mm.) for the back and
    18 in. x 24 in. (457 x 610 mm.) for the base.

2   Cut members for back frame from 18 mm x 37 mm planed softwood as
    follows: 2 pieces 28 in. (711 mm.) long with one end mitred; 1 piece
    19 in. (483 mm.) long with both ends mitred; 1 piece 16 in. (406 mm.)
    long with both ends square.

3   Glue and pin frames together centrally on backboard leaving
    approximately 3 in. (76 mm.) margin to sides and top. Frames should
    project approximately ¾ in. (19 mm.) at bottom.

4   Cut members for base frame from 18 mm. x 37 mm. planed softwood
    as follows: 2 pieces 20 in. (508 mm.) long with one end mitred; 1 piece
    22 in. (559 mm.) long with both ends mitred; 2 pieces 19 in. (483 mm.)
    long with both ends square. Cut 1 piece from 25 mm. x 25 mm. planed
    softwood for backstop 22 in. (559 mm.) long with both ends half jointed
    37 mm. x 18 mm.

5   Drill a 6 mm. diameter hole in the 18 mm. faces of the 22 in. (559 mm.)
    long cross-braces 2 in. (51 mm.) from each end. Make certain that the
    holes are central on the wood and are drilled at right angles to the face
    of the wood.

6   Glue and pin frame together centrally on baseboard leaving
    approximately 1 in. (25 mm.) margin to front and sides. The frames
    should project approximately 3 in. (76 mm.) beyond the back of the
    baseboard. Fix one of the crossbraces level with the rear edge of the
    baseboard and the second 9 in. (229 m.) nearer the front. Ensure that
    the projecting frame of the backboard fits easily between the projecting
    frames of the baseboard.

7   Insert the bent steel rods into the holes in the crossbraces so that they
    will rotate as shown on the diagram.

8   Fix backstop 1 in. (25 mm.) from rear edge of the baseboard.

9   Fix 6 mm. Terry clips on inside of backboard frames approximately
    10 in. (254 mm.) from bottom edge.

10 When you are satisfied that the assembly will fit together correctly,
    ensuring that there is sufficient clearance between the backboard and
    the baseboard for two thicknesses of the selected wallpaper or material,
    rub down any rough places with sandpaper.

11 Cover backboard and baseboard with selected wallpaper or material
    and allow to dry laying flat to prevent warping.

12 Colour to suit proposed exhibit.

DRAPES

Drapes are not used so frequently now as they were some years ago but they can still play their part. There are certain classes which are enhanced by the use of a correct drape which can produce the necessary atmosphere in a period design, link separate placements, emphasize a line, or conceal staging such as tins, wood blocks or even a book which has been used to give added height to one of the components. Drapes may be placed at the back of your exhibit and be arranged so that all the components stand on them, or they may be used purely as background.

As for bases and backgrounds, the correct choice of texture, colour and fabric for drapes is of the utmost importance, because drapes must not be more dominant than the plant material. The use of patterned, shiny or bright fabrics should be avoided as this leads to confusion. In order to emphasize your arrangement choose a light-colour drape behind dark plant material, and a darker tone behind light-coloured plant material. A slightly shiny-surfaced drape is often better used with dull-surfaced plant material, but your texture must be chosen according to your class title and the flowers. For example hessian, tweed, hopsack or a heavy weave should be used with wild flowers, marigolds, fruit and vegetables or a landscape. But to indicate tranquillity and romance, use a delicate rayon, chiffon or crepe teamed with sweet peas and small roses. Velvet gives a feeling of antiquity and elegance.

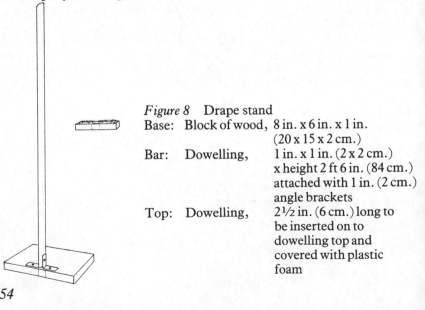

Figure 8 Drape stand
Base: Block of wood, 8 in. x 6 in. x 1 in.
(20 x 15 x 2 cm.)
Bar: Dowelling, 1 in. x 1 in. (2 x 2 cm.)
x height 2 ft 6 in. (84 cm.)
attached with 1 in. (2 cm.)
angle brackets
Top: Dowelling, 2½ in. (6 cm.) long to
be inserted on to
dowelling top and
covered with plastic
foam

54

Allow two metres of the best quality material you can afford because cheap material rarely enhances the plant material and does not fall well. Nylon-jersey, crepe and chiffon are excellent because they fall into graceful folds. Position the drape in the niche or space before starting to arrange your plant material. Unless the schedule states otherwise the ends may be gathered into a bulldog clip and hung over the back of the niche, so that the clip acts as a counterbalance.

A drape stand may be bought or made quite simply by sinking a piece of dowel 2 ft 6 in. (84 cm.) long into a block of wood 8 in. x 6 in. x 1 in. (20 cm. x 15 cm. x 2 cm.) (see figure 8). To prevent the top from being too pointed a smaller piece of dowel 2½ in. (6 cm.) long may be attached to the top and covered with plastic foam, giving a softer line when the fabric is placed over it. The container or one of the other components can be placed on the base to steady it.

TITLE OF EXHIBIT

When your exhibit needs a title, it should not be scribbled on a piece of paper at the last moment. After all, it is an accessory and should be chosen and styled with as much care and attention as all the other components. It should be well written, suitable in style (Letraset may be used if calligraphy is not your strong point), and on suitable material, for example, stone or bark for woodland, bamboo for oriental. White card should be used with care as it is extremely eye catching and a quick brush over with tea or coffee helps to make the card less dominant.

To enable the card to be self supporting, the following method may be used (see figure 9). You need a piece of card, preferably

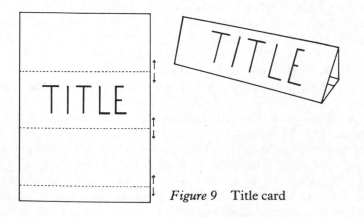

Figure 9 Title card

coloured to match the flowers, background or drape, measuring 5 in. x 4 in. (12 cm. x 10 cm.), or in these proportions, according to the size of your exhibit. Fold 1½ in. (3.5 cm.) down from the 4 in. (10 cm.) edge, then fold again 1½ in. (3.5 cm.) below that fold and finally 1½ in. (3.5 cm.) below that, leaving a lip of ½ in. (1.5 cm.). Your wording should now be written between the first and second fold on the outside, and, when the lettering is dry, the lip should be stuck under the top, forming a triangle which cannot fall over. Press the lip to the underside by means of a piece of stick inserted through the centre.

PLANT MATERIAL

Finally we come to the most important item of your exhibit – the plant material. This must be of appropriate colour, texture and shape for the class in which it is to be used.

Flowers and foliage

The colour of your plant material plays a very important part in interpreting a mood or creating the right atmosphere. Red for example denotes heat, gaiety, passion, love, anger, and feeling of carnival or Christmas; grey, mauve and purple give a feeling of melancholy, twilight or seascape, and recall the Victorian era; green suggests coolness, freshness, tranquility, and a woodland atmosphere and it also represents jealousy; white stands for purity, coldness and honesty; while pinks, pale blue, cream and apricot hint at fragile beauty; yellow gives a feeling of sun, cheerfulness, youth and candlelight; while orange suggests autumn, sun, happiness and heat; blue, being cold, represents space, sea and sky.

Your choice of the texture and shape of the flowers and foliage is not quite so important as their colour, although texture, too, plays its part in creating atmosphere. A rough, dull texture gives a feeling of strength and melancholy; a shiny one depicts festivity and sophistication; whilst a smooth, downy one conveys femininity and elegance.

Next we must consider the shape of your plant material, which can be divided into three basic groups: pointed, round, and 'in-between'.

The pointed or delicate, which are used to outline your exhibit, include Phormium tenax, alder, small-leaved foliage such as privet, beech, branches of trees in bud or just blossoming, grasses, verbascum seed heads, liatris, gladioli, larkspur, foxglove, delphinium, molucella, antirrhinum, broom, montbretia, spray carnations, and trailing ivy, honeysuckle and vinca.

The round, solid forms which are dominant, and are therefore usually placed at the centre and base of the exhibit, are roses, carnations, chrysanthemums, paeonies, gerbera, anthuriums, geranium flowers and leaves, begonia rex, alchimilla leaves, hosta leaves, angelica seed heads and bergenia leaves.

Finally, there are the 'in-betweens' or transition material which is used to create a gradual change from the delicate and pointed to the large and solid. Amongst these are the flowers of the alchemilla, hydrangea (depending on colour) and bergenia, and the foliage of choisya, cupressus, ferns, viburnum and skimmia.

Certain moods and ideas may be created as follows:
bountifulness can be suggested by fruit, marigolds, gladioli, dahlias and zinnias; **the countryside** by driftwood, ivy, ferns, wild material, daisy chrysanthemums, arum leaves and foxgloves; **drama** by driftwood, orchids, zinnias, strelitzia, anthuriums, hot-house foliage, fatsia, lillies and allium seed heads; **elegance and grace** by cytisus praecox, eucalyptus, grevillia, bocconia, roses, carnations and honeysuckle; **mists and shadows** by begonia foliage, anemones, bare branches, lichen, grey foliage, poppy seed heads and driftwood; **love, romance and fantasy** by using camellias, lilac, stocks, sweet peas, roses, spray carnations, grevillia and freesias; **the sea** by chlorophytum, succulents, onopordium, echinops, scabious, irises and driftwood; and **tranquillity and peace** by camellias, lilies, magnolias, and paeonies.

When selecting your plant material make certain there are no special restrictions or requests governing your class. For example, a bud showing colour or variegated foliage would be disastrous in an 'All Green' class.

Fruit

More and more varieties of fruit are becoming available in the shops throughout the year so there should be no difficulty linking the colour of your fruit to your flowers and foliage. This is important because your fruit must be an integral part of your exhibit.

To help it stay in position it can be placed on rubber bands from jam jars, which will prevent it from rolling, or it can be given a false stem by pressing half a cocktail stick into the fruit and the other half into the water-retaining foam, or into another piece of fruit (see figure 10). Heavier fruit such as pineapples or melons need something stronger than a cocktail stick to anchor them. One or two

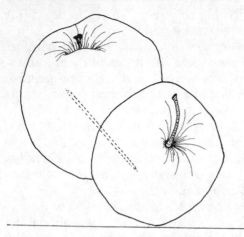

Figure 10 Apples joined with skewers

Figure 11 Pineapple with skewers

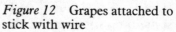

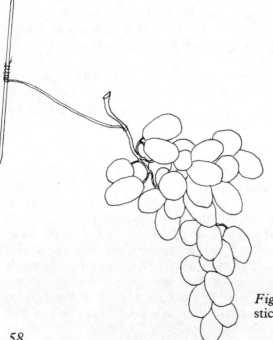

Figure 12 Grapes attached to stick with wire

wooden meat skewers or kebab sticks are ideal for this (see figure 11). Grapes may be anchored by attaching a short piece of stick to the stem of the bunch with stub wire (see figure 12).

Fir cones, which are also considered to be fruit, can be given a false stem by using a stub wire and winding it round the bottom of the cone, under the lower scales if possible. This gives it a good anchorage and prevents the wire from slipping. Bring the two 'legs' of wire together, one slightly longer than the other, and wind the longer of the two round the shorter. The heavier the cone the thicker the stub wire required. Nuts, which are also classified as fruit, should have two small holes bored or drilled into their shells and wired in the same manner as for fir cones.

Driftwood

The best things in life are free and this applies to the beautiful driftwood, twisted roots, gnarled branches and even pieces of tree stumps which are to be found in the woods and hedges, on the moors and heaths, along the riverbanks and sea shores, or on the bonfire. Driftwood is of course plant material and not an accessory, but it cannot be used in a class requiring fresh plant material as it is classified as dried plant material, so make sure you read your schedule carefully.

Searching for driftwood gives added interest to flower arranging, but a little work needs to be done before it can be used in an exhibit. Very few pieces can be used just as they were found without undergoing some cleaning and preparation. The soft, rotting parts should be removed with a small pointed knife, so that only hard wood is left. This can then be scrubbed in detergent and water to which a little disinfectant has been added to remove the unwanted insects as well as the dirt. It should be allowed to dry, preferably in the sun, after which it should be given a hard brush with a wire brush. The only exception to this treatment is grey driftwood and for this, the minimum of scrubbing and brushing is advocated. A soft brush only should be used otherwise the wood will lose its lovely grey colouring. When some of the rotten wood has been removed, small cavitites may be left which can be adapted to take a small container for your plant material.

You may wish to trim or join two or three pieces of similar wood by either gluing or screwing them together. Your wood may be given a sheen with colourless furniture or shoe polish, which should be well rubbed in and left for 24 hours to allow time for it to soak into the wood before being polished. Coloured shoe polish may also be used if a change of shade is desired, or the wood can be darkened by using linseed oil. On the other hand, you may prefer to bleach it by soaking it in a bucket containing half water and half household bleach. It is better not to use varnish, even matt varnish, as this takes away some of the wood's natural look.

Keep an eye open for branches of gorse or heather which have survived a heath fire. They are dirty so are best collected when wearing old clothes and gloves. By immersing them in a bucket or tub of water and giving them a good scrub, they will clean up completely without leaving deposits of soot every time they are handled. As an extra precaution, when they are dry rub them over with colourless shoe polish.

The smaller pieces of wood can easily be fixed onto a pinholder by splitting the end of the stem before pressing it on to the pins. If you think the stems are too big and heavy to be put into water-retaining foam, they can be treated in the same manner as candles and given false legs using thin garden cane instead of cocktail sticks.

If you are one of the unfortunate people who never find a suitable piece of driftwood, you can enjoy preparing freshly cut branches of tree ivy, honeysuckle, wisteria or vine. The outside bark should be stripped, the branch placed in cold water to soak for at least 24 hours (the rain water butt is ideal for this), after which it should easily loop or curve into whatever shape you want. It may then be fastened securely into shape with string or clothes pegs until it has dried.

Driftwood can be used any time of the year, and because there are no two pieces alike, each exhibit must be different. It needs to be anchored firmly in one of the following ways.

1 Clamps will be needed for the larger, heavier pieces. These are obtainable at good florists or your local flower club. These have a reversed pinholder with a screw which holds the wood firmly even when it is angled to one side. This then fits on to an ordinary pinholder and is hiddeen by your plant material.

2 The driftwood may be screwed on to a wooden base which is a more permanent method. Do not fit it immediately you have finished cleaning and treating it. Prop it up in different positions and have a good look at it from various angles before deciding which one you prefer. You will probably find that the end of the stem is too long or it needs levelling to make it stand flat on the base at the angle you have chosen. To obtain an accurate cutting line, put the end into a bowl of water, holding it at the desired angle and lowering it into the water until you have the required height. When removed you should have a waterline indicating the correct place for you to cut. Once cut

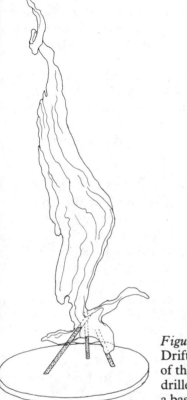

Figure 13
Driftwood supported on dowel 'false legs'. Holes of the same diameter as the dowel have been drilled into the driftwood, which is standing on a base

it is ready to fix on to a wood slice or a block of wood. This should have had a long screw countersunk and inserted through it so that the screw projects upwards and your driftwood can be fastened onto it.
3 It may be necessary to add false legs of dowel for balance (see figure 13). Two of these are usually sufficient, the main leg being the wood itself. Drill the required number of holes into the driftwood the same diameter as the dowel, then insert the dowel, cut to the required length. A spot of glue may be necessary if the dowel is loose, but the weight of the wood should hold it in position. It may then be stood on a base or inserted on to a pinholder.
4 An alternative method is to give your wood a ring of false legs by binding short lengths of garden cane, kebab sticks or wooden meat skewers round the end with oasis tape or wire. These should then be inserted into the water-retaining foam. Extra support may be given by using two or three cocktail sticks as wedges, putting them into the

foam as close to the wood as possible.

5 To hold your driftwood at an angle, anchor it to the base by taking green plastic covered wire through the base and around the wood. This method was employed in the landscape exhibit (illustration 10).

Driftwood has many uses. It can be very dramatic and dominant used in a modern or abstract exhibit, but can also play a less conspicuous role in a landscape or seascape, by creating the necessary atmosphere and becoming part of the outline. Smaller pieces and chunks of driftwood are useful for hiding your mechanics and containers.

A MOCK-UP

Until you become more experienced you may find it helpful to have a mock-up or trial run at home, but for this to be of any benefit you must use the same space as the one you will be using at the show. Make an improvised niche using a large cardboard box cut to the correct size, giving it the all important 'wings' or side pieces. If you work in a shed or garage you may prefer to mark the wall behind the table or bench, also drawing a line either side on the table top to make sure your exhibit is not too wide. This will tell you whether your exhibit is too tall or not tall enough, whether you have filled your space well but not over- or under-filled it, and, most important, whether your exhibit interprets your class title well. If it does not, or if it is too big or too small, you have time at this stage to think again.

A mock-up also prevents you from wasting precious time when you arrive at the show and gives you more confidence in knowing where and how best to use your drape, where to place your container, whether your accessories are in scale, how many to use, whether your choice of container is suitable for the class title and for your plant material, whether your base is too big, too small, the wrong colour or the wrong material, and whether your well-conditioned plant material predominates over all else.

You may have taken all these points into consideration, but how do you know whether your exhibit is good, bad or indifferent? Perhaps answering the following questions will be of help.

1 Does the whole present a pleasing picture? If it does not, is something out of scale, too dominant or nothing sufficiently dominant? Are the flowers in scale with each other, with the container, and with the space allowed?

2 Are all the components to scale? This is very essential particularly in miniature and petite exhibits.

3 Have you contrasting shapes in the foliage?

4 Is the exhibit well balanced? Remember that balance can be obtained with colour as well as plant material. White is a very dominant colour; your eye is drawn to it and it is often used near the centre. A traditional exhibit should appear light in weight at the top and outside, and heavier towards the bottom and centre.

5 Is your container the correct size? Always remember your container should never predominate. It is far better to have it on the small size rather than the large.

6 Are your bases well covered and clean; your drapes crease-free with no frayed edges showing; your background firmly fixed, well painted or covered?

7 Are your accessories appropriate, to scale and well grouped?

8 Have you chosen a suitable container and plant material for the title? If for example, the class is 'The Promise of Spring' avoid using flowers from the florist, such as carnations or roses, which although they are available in the shop, are either green-house grown or imported, and more suited to summer. Instead, use spring bulbs with a branch of blossom just on the point of opening so that its buds give a promise of the spring to come. Choose a simple container. Spring blossoms and flowers look lovely arranged on a slice of wood in an empty food tin which has been hidden by the use of stones, moss, bark or fungus.

9 If you are using a secondary placement, the movement in your first placement should lead the eye to it. Check whether it does.

If most of your answers are 'yes', you have done your best to ensure your exhibit will do you credit.

6. Preparing your flowers and foliage

Conditioning

The most important preparation of all is conditioning your plant material, which means taking steps to ensure it can obtain the maximum amount of water possible from the moment it is cut. Never skimp on the time you spend on this most necessary job, because your plant material must stand for the entire show and not just until your exhibit has been judged. Your drapes may be well pressed, your bases beautifully covered, backgrounds well painted and then your material lets you down and wilts because it has been incorrectly or insufficiently conditioned. All your time, effort and money will have been wasted because many, many marks will be lost for wilting plant material.

Why does plant material need conditioning for so long if it is to be arranged in water? The reason for giving it something more than just a quick drink is to acclimatise the plant material to the changed atmosphere. It is brought in from a damp, chilly environment where it is able to absorb moisture through its leaves as well as stems into a warm, dry one. It needs, therefore to take up as much water as possible before being arranged and to continue to take up moisture afterwards. It is far better to leave your plant material in deep water for a few hours more rather than less. If you think your time will be limited the day before the show, gather or purchase your flowers and foliage a day earlier. Another 24 hours will do them no harm.

CUTTING YOUR PLANT MATERIAL

First of all make certain your buckets and scissors are clean – very clean. Bacteria in the water from dirty buckets will clog the cut ends of the stems and prevent them from taking up moisture. It is best to gather your plant material in the evening or early morning when transpiration is at its lowest, cutting the stems on the slant to create a greater area for the absorption of water. Cut your flowers at various stages of development, some buds, some half-open flowers and some blooms.

1 Competitors staging at a NAFAS competition: different types of staging and their coverings may be seen.

Tables in the centre of the hall have been skirted in muslin using knife-pleating. The tops are covered with felt, and pelmets in the same material have been attached to the skirting with double-sided adhesive tape. Pelmets may also be seen on the large square bases at each side of the photograph. 'Throw-over' coverings have been used on the rows of individual circular platforms.

Class titles and notices such as 'Photography' have been staged on poles which have been bound with ribbon, and set into tins of cement the top and sides of which were covered in fabric.

2   Preparing the staging. Laminate-topped tables have their sides draped with fabric, which is attached to the top of the table with adhesive tape. Electric conduit and fabric are used for the background. The conduit was sunk into coffee tins painted the same colour as the fabric and filled with cement. These can be seen between the table legs.

3   Table support. Two pieces of chipboard are slotted into each other to form the support for any type of top. These particular pieces are being used to support an individual platform, but if the chipboard is cut taller it may be used for table-height tops.

4 Exhibits staged on circular bases, the tops of which have been covered in fabric before the sides are attached. The sides were made of card and covered with the same fabric as the top, as described in Chapter 2 (Island Sites). Also shown is an alternative method for displaying class titles well above the heads of the public, enabling them to be easily read.

In the background may be seen a different type of staging – individual alcoves 3 ft. deep and 6 ft. high with lighting for each exhibit concealed by the pelmet at the top.

5 'Anniversary', staged by Dorothy Monks.

An exhibit for a buffet table featuring red roses to be staged against a burgundy-coloured background was called for. The variegated foliage of astrantia and ivy has been used to lighten the arrangement, whilst *Berberis thunbergii* links with the colour of the background. Grapes, green apples and *Alchemilla mollis* have also been used. The arrangements were staged on bases covered in burgundy-coloured velvet, bright red candles providing a link with the red roses.

6 'Garden of Love', staged by Dorothy Morgan.

The lovely white foxgloves and bracken create the atmosphere of the garden, whilst the lilies and roses are indicative of romance. The figurine and fruit help to depict the Garden of Eden.

7 'After Dark', staged by Susan Phillips.

Here a candle-lit dinner interprets the title. The background and curtain in strong peacock blue and the careful grouping of a few well-chosen accessories immediately create the atmosphere and tell you exactly what the exhibit portrays. The plant material is in shades of yellow and orange and includes galdioli, carnations, roses, lilies and variagated weigelia, as well as some fruit. The pale turquoise candles complete a well-staged exhibit.

8 'Christmas Canticle', staged by Winifred Simpson.

This exhibit together with 'Northern Contrasts' (see opposite) illustrate two different types of background. In this exhibit a shaded background shows to advantage the gold figure, gilded curling driftwood and gold flowers used to interpret the quotation 'My Soul doth magnify the Lord'.

9 'Northern Contrasts', staged by Mollie Duerr.

In this exhibit a painted background helps to portray the industrial North, whilst the driftwood, bracken and white daisies represent the lovely countryside so different from the unsightly factories and tall chimneys on the background.

10   Using driftwood

Stage I: Driftwood is anchored by means of green plastic-covered wire taken through the base and around the wood, holding the wood at an angle.

Stage II: Placing the containers for flowers and foliage.

Stage III: The finished exhibit using spring flowers with birds and nest as accessories.

11 'Ich Dien – I Serve', staged by Mary Brett-Dodds, Zoë Moore and Joan Toley. A group exhibit, interpreting the title by depicting the Fire Service.

Staged on a grey-coloured base, blackened driftwood, pampas grass and grey foliage represent the smoke, while gladioli, spray carnations, roses, lilies, and gerbera in shades of orange to red depict the fire at its height. The clever use of the seed heads of *Phormium tenax*, red anthuriums, and orange lilies with the bark of Pandanus curling through the arrangement tells you at once that the flames have been almost extinguished leaving behind the charred remains.

12 'Still Life', staged by Dorothy Monks.

13 'The Plant Hunters', staged by Winifred Simpson.

A Pot-et-Fleur using a figurine and imported plant material such as African violets, cyclamen, tradescantia, maranta and cut orchids in a pink, mauve and grey colouring, arranged in a shallow dish.

14 'A Man For All Seasons', staged by Elspeth Hamilton.
A Pot-et-Fleur using sansevieria, begonia, chlorophytum, sedum and roses arranged in a lidded picnic basket.

15 'Garden of Love', staged by Robert Barlow.

Here we have a still-life with plant material predominating. Staged on a marble base, driftwood representing the serpent in the Garden of Eden is included in the top arrangement which is raised on a plinth masked at one side by a red drape, whilst red apples and purple grapes grouped at the base carry the theme and the pink and red colouring through the exhibit. The plant material includes honeysuckle, roses, echeveria, vine and the seed heads of allium and poppy.

16 'The Romanies', staged by Mrs S. Coulthard.

Wild and simple plant material combine to portray the title. Bracken, grasses, foxgloves, scabious and daisies are arranged in a basket out of which tumble lace and ribbons.

17 'Poetry of Love', staged by Gerry Reid.

The delicate shading of pink and grey and choice of plant material bears out the title of the poem 'She Walks in Beauty'. Pink drapes covered with grey chiffon link the two arrangements. Astilbe roses, carnations, lilies, astrantia, and gerbera in shades of pink combine with grey foliages such as *Stachy's lanata*, senecio, *Cineraria maritima*, *Rosa rubrifolia*, and *Begonia rex* to create this beautiful exhibit. (Opposite)

18 'Sanctuary', staged by Diana Joyce.

The Sanctuary portrayed in this exhibit is a Wild Butterfly Sanctuary and all the plant material used is favoured by butterflies for its nectar. Wild and semi-wild plant material in mixed pastel shades include foxgloves, penstemon, honeysuckle, sweet william, grasses and dandelion seed-heads which have been carefully sprayed with hair lacquer to prevent them from shattering.

Take a bucket of water with you so that the stems may be placed in water as soon as possible. This prevents the cut ends from drying over and restricting their water intake. This is especially important when cutting material such as cow-parsley or dock from the hedgerows. Foliage, pussy willow, catkins and other material found in woods and hedges should be cut carefully with scissors. Don't take too much and never cut or use protected plant material.

Once you have gathered all your flowers and foliage, some stems will need special treatment before being put into buckets of warm water and left overnight. The following methods have been tried, tested and found to work. If time is very limited and you really do not have the opportunity of giving your plant material a long soak, there is a product which can be obtained from florists called Chrysal which does help. Your water-retaining foam should be soaked in the solution before being used.

SUBMERGING

The reason for submerging foliage is that moisture is taken in through the leaves as well as through the stems. The final 1 in. (2.5 cm.) of the stems of very young foliage should be plunged into boiling water then submerged in a bowl of tepid water for a maximum of two hours, whereas old foliage may be left submerged overnight. Hostas, Arum italicum pictum, young ivy leaves, paeony leaves, and even bergenia leaves benefit from being submerged at any stage of their development. But grey leaves such as Senecio greyei and Cineraria maritima are the exception. They become waterlogged and lose their grey colour.

BOILING

This serves two purposes. It kills bacteria and breaks through any seal or airlock, enabling water to be drawn up the stem. It is particularly useful for young foliage, woody stems, wilted flowers and roses. The stems should be held in 1 in. (2.5 cm.) of boiling water for up to one minute, the flower heads being protected from the steam by wrapping them in a cloth or plastic bag (figure 14). They should then be submerged or left to soak.

BURNING

When cutting poppies, bocconia or any of the euphorbias, a milky liquid will seep from the cut end. To prevent this from becoming

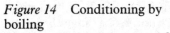

Figure 14 Conditioning by boiling

A rose, with head protected from steam by plastic or piece of cloth wrapped round it, inserted into 2 in. of boiling water for up to one minute.

Figure 15 Hollow stem

Funnel inserted into upturned stem of delphinium for easy filling with water rubbery and sealing over the end of the stem, hold the end in a lighted match or candle and count to 30, then place in deep warm water. Be very careful when handling euphorbia, avoid getting the milky liquid on your face or near your eyes as it can be very harmful.

FILLING HOLLOW STEMS

Hollow stems such as those of lupins, delphiniums, foxgloves and large dahlias may be filled with water by inserting a small funnel in the end of the stem (figure 15), by using a large dropper and then plugging the end of the stem with cotton wool which acts as a wick, or by holding your thumb over the end of the stem to prevent the water from coming out until you have placed the flower in a bucket of tepid water. An improvised funnel can be made by cutting the top from a washing-up liquid container 2 in. (5 cm.) from the top. Discard the bottom or use it for making a container.

SOAKING

Any very woody stems should have their ends split at least 2 in. (5 cm.) up from the ends and a little of the outside bark scraped away to allow a larger area for water absorption. They should then be placed in a bucket of warm water to which a few drops of household bleach or disinfectant has been added. The use of starch in the water has proved to be beneficial when using some type of leaves, especially ferns and arum. Mix a heaped tablespoon of starch with a minimum of four pints of water.

RETARDING DEVELOPMENT

You may find it useful to retard the development of some of your plant material. It is possible to keep paeonies and gladioli for a week by picking when the buds are just showing colour, leaving them out of water on a stone floor, or in a flower box with the lid on. When the flowers are required, cut their ends and put them in warm water. Garden flowers picked in bud can be prevented from opening too quickly by plunging them into a bucket of ice-cold water and standing it in a cool dark place.

If you obtain your flowers from a florist, they will probably all be at the same stage of development. In order to keep some in bud and bring others out, the following method may be followed. Cut ½ in. (1 cm.) from the ends of the stems and leave in deep water for about two hours. Remove as many buds as you require and tie into a plastic bag, place in the refrigerator until required. This works particularly well with roses, carnations and chrysanthemums. Leave those required at the half-opened stage in water in a cold room, whilst those needed as blooms should be put into a warm room.

FORCING DEVELOPMENT

Branches of flowering shrubs such as chaenomeles, forsythia, Garrya elliptica, kerria, prunus, ribes, salix and syringa may be cut and forced into bloom much earlier than if left in the garden. They should be picked when the large buds appear. Hammer their stems and place in deep, warm water in a really warm room, or stand near the boiler and spray with warm water from time to time to soften the bud scales. This may take as long as three to four weeks, so if they are needed for a special occasion allow plenty of time. If development becomes too rapid, remove from a warm to a cool room.

WILTED FLOWERS

If you find that one of your flowers has wilted overnight, this indicates that it is not taking up water. It may be revived by cutting about 2 in. (5 cm.) from the end of the stem under water, thus removing the air bubble. Leave in deep, warm water for at least two hours.

Roses should always have the end of the stems cut and placed in 2 in. (5 cm.) of boiling water while the heads are protected from the steam by being wrapped loosely in tissue or kitchen paper. After one minute, remove from the boiling water and float the whole stem and flower in a bowl of water.

DRIED AND PRESERVED PLANT MATERIAL

Treatment for plant material which has been dried or preserved with glycerine is also very important if you are using it in water. In this case you will want to prevent it from, rather than to encourage it to take up moisture. If the stems are in water for any length of time they will become soft and decay. To prevent this happening and also to stop moisture being absorbed up the stem, dip the ends of the stems in nail varnish or melted candle wax. When dismantling your exhibit be sure to dry your preserved plant material thoroughly before storing it to prevent decay.

The seed heads of bullrushes, clematis and pampas grass should be sprayed with hair lacquer to prevent them from bursting.

PLANTS NEEDING SPECIAL TREATMENT

Because it is so important to ensure your plant material has been well prepared, listed below are some of the plants which require special treatment, together with the appropriate treatment for each of them.

Acanthus leaves: dip ends of stems in boiling water and then submerge in weak starch water overnight.

Anemone: dip stems in boiling water. Avoid arranging it in water-retaining foam.

Angelica: does not always respond to boiling and soaking. It lasts better when seed heads are formed.

Artichoke leaves: unlike other grey leaves boil ends of stems, and submerge overnight. It is helpful to bind the stem end to prevent it from splitting.

Berberis thunbergii: top and tail by nipping the top off the stem and peel the bark from the end before placing in deep water.

Carnations: always cut between the nodes. Standing in fizzy lemonade works wonders if the stems are weak.

Caenothus: does not last however well it is conditioned

Clematis: remove all leaves and submerge flowers for approximately one hour.

Dahlias: are easily bruised. Burn the cut ends of the stems and, if large, fill the hollow stems with water.

Florists' flowers (or flowers bought direct from the flower market): need to be untied or unwrapped from the bunch in which they have been sold. Cut 1 in. (2.5 cm.) from the stems, remove the lower leaves, and place in deep tepid water.

Gerberas: seal cut stems with a flame or with boiling water before plunging into deep, tepid water up to the flowers. They will take up water better if the ends of the stems are not allowed to touch the bottom of the bucket. A mound of wire netting put over the top of the bucket and the stems threaded through this will help to suspend them in the water.

Hellebores: can be very tricky if used before seed heads are formed. Boil the ends of the stems, then make a shallow incision with a sharp, pointed knife, or pin the entire length of the stem starting as near the flower head as possible. Immerse the whole of the stems in water for several hours. They will last much better if arranged in deep rather than shallow water, with stems as short as possible.

Hyacinths: stand in a bucket on their own for about two hours until the thick sap, which damages other flowers, has seeped from the stem.

Hydrangeas: immerse flower heads in water for a minimum of one hour, but no longer than overnight otherwise they become transparent. They will last longer if cut when the heads are mature.

Lamium maculatum: place ends in boiling water then leave submerged in cold water for at least 12 hours. They will then last perfectly giving excellent trailing sprays of very pretty foliage.

Lilac (see syringa)

Narcissi (Daffodil): two or three drops of washing-up liquid in the water is beneficial. Always arrange in a shallow container as they do not like deep water. If the stem ends split, bind with wool which, unlike string or wire, does not cut the stems.

Rhus cotinus purpurens: must have the ends of the stems boiled then totally submerged for several hours.

Roses: place 1 in. (2.5 cm.) of each stem in a jug of boiling water, count to 20, then fill the jug with cold water and leave for four hours. Protect the flower heads from steam by wrapping in tissue or kitchen paper. Hot water may cause the stems to become floppy, so cut them off before arranging.

Sansevieria: do not put into water as the stems become soggy. Mount on false legs (as for candles) by binding two or three cocktail sticks round the base of the stem with tape or wool, and inserting these into the water-retaining foam or pinholder leaving the end of the stem just above the water. The false legs must be concealed by other plant material for show work.

Syringa (lilac): remove all foliage to make the flowers last longer and display better. Cut a few non-flowering branches if leaves are required. Split the ends of the stems, leave for several hours in warm water, and arrange with flowering stems.

Stachys lanata: leaves will act as a syphon if allowed to get too wet.

Tellima: Cut, but do not pick the leaves so that the tenuous thread inside the stem is neatly severed with the stalk, then submerge for several hours.

Tulips: wrap tightly in newspaper and stand in deep, cold water.

Vinca: nip tops from stems and submerge.

Vitis: foliage must be mature when cut and should be singed, followed by a brief soaking in tepid water.

Zinnias: immerse heads in water for 15 minutes before placing the ends of the stems in boiling water and leaving in warm water overnight. Large blooms with hollow stems should be filled with warm water, or alternatively may have a stub wire inserted up the stem for extra support. No wires should be visible in show work.

7. Staging your Exhibit

TRANSPORTING YOUR EQUIPMENT

Make a list of everything you will need to take to the show with you. It might appear long and formidable, you may not need it all, but it is a useful check list as you are packing your car. It should include: a suitable container; well-conditioned plant material; accessories (if allowed); drapes/background/bases; mechanics, i.e., water-retaining foam, pinholders, wire netting, tape or elastic bands; scissors; knife (to cut water-retaining foam and for scraping ends of stems); watering can and spray; bucket/s; show schedule; reel wire and stub wires (to strengthen stems); tubes and cones (for added height); rubber rings and cocktail sticks (if using fruit or vegetables); sheet of polythene on which to work; small cloth or towel to mop up spillage.

The easiest and most convenient way of transporting your plant material to the show is in buckets, each exhibit being sorted separately. This saves time when you arrive because you will not have plant material to unpack, stems to re-cut and buckets to fill with water before you can begin staging. It may be possible to pack the car so that the buckets are wedged firmly and will not fall over, but it is far safer to use an easily made carrier for either two or four buckets (figure 16). To carry four buckets you need:
6 pieces of wood ½ in. x ½ in. x 20 in. (1½ cm. x 1½ cm. x 50 cm.)
4 pieces of wood 1 in. x 5 in. x 4 in. (2½ cm. x 12 cm. x 10 cm.)
13 1½-in. (4 cm.) screws.
Join together as illustrated. An alternative method is to use a firm box from the florist with two holes cut into it (figure 17).

Fasten large platstic bags over the tops of your buckets to help retain the moisture, and put a large pinholder in the bottom of each bucket for stability. A milk-bottle carrier containing large empty coffee jars is also a very useful way to carry smaller flowers and precious leaves.

If preferred, flower boxes may be used instead of buckets. Well-conditioned flowers and foliage, carefully packed and left undisturbed, will keep quite happily for up to two days in a box which has had the base and sides *only* lined with thin plastic sheeting,

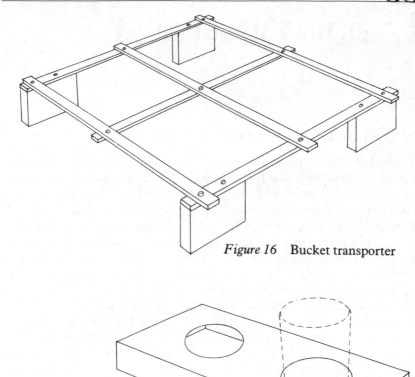

Figure 16   Bucket transporter

Figure 17   Bucket carrier using a florist box
Cut two holes very slightly larger than base of bucket

covered by a layer of damp newspaper or tissue paper. Arrange the heavy blooms so that the heads are not on top of one another. The box will travel better if full, and spaces may be filled with either damp tissue paper, kitchen roll or lightweight foliage. The contents should then be given a final spray and covered with a slightly damp sheet of tissure paper, *not* plastic, before closing the lid. Keep the box as level as possible in transit, and leave it unopened until the contents are required. Before fixing your drapes and preparing your staging, re-cut stems and place in buckets of water to enable them to have a good drink whilst you are arranging your accessories. Make use of the individual stem tubes which are supplied when buying anthuriums or orchids from the florist. Pack your more delicate blooms in these.

When using geraniums or rhododendrons pack with all leaves still on the stem as these protect the flower heads in transit, then remove unwanted leaves before arranging. The tips of flowers with spikes, such as delphiniums, gladioli, foxgloves, larkspur and lupins, tend to curl when laid horizontally for any length of time, so if you are undertaking a journey of several hours they are best placed in buckets, unless you require curly-tipped delphiniums, etc.

Foliage should be packed in plastic bags with the open ends tied up to hold in the moisture. But take care that your grey foliage is not left too long like this otherwise it will lose its colour.

Wrap your containers and accessories in newspaper or thin plastic foam sheeting before putting into a basket or box. Cover your backgrounds, bases and roll of drapes with an old piece of sheeting or clean plastic. Pack your car carefully, checking that everything has been put in. Organize the family meals so you can be off with an easy mind.

USING YOUR TIME SENSIBLY

Make sure you leave enough time for your journey so that you arrive at the hall in plenty of time. Before removing anything from your car, discover where your entries are to be staged and where the water supply is located. Unpack your car and get your plant material into water, then put your background or drapes into position and your container in place with the mechanics firmly fixed so that you are ready to begin.

Allow yourself time at the end of arranging your exhibit to walk away, perhaps stage your second entry, or look at the other exhibits. Do not look at the work of other competitors in your class before you start because you might be tempted to change your ideas which is never beneficial.

Come back, stand back, and you can then assess your work with fresh eyes. If you cannot see obvious mistakes, such as plant material not in water, mechanics showing, or having exceeded your given space, leave your exhibit alone. Do not fiddle with it as this could result in your water-retaining foam crumbling leaving you with no time to start all over again. Check that all containers, including cones and tubes have plenty of water and are not leaking, and that no leaves are acting as a syphon for the water in your container. Then spray your plant material, taking care not to wet your drapes and accessories.

Giving your finished exhibit a good spray is very important. So many exhibition halls have air-conditioning which is not kind to plant material as it lacks humidity. Halls and marquees are usually warm, especially in summer, whilst cathedrals and churches, although cold, are inclined to draw the moisture from the exhibits. By spraying you are increasing the moisture content of the air and so reducing transpiration from the leaves.

Gather up your rubbish, but don't include your competitor's class card with it. This is easily done, and it is annoying for the hard-working competition secretary when she has to make a new one at the last moment just at the time she should be greeting the judge. So spare a thought for her. Also have some consideration for the stewards who will be undertaking the watering. Do not pack your water-retaining foam so tightly that they are unable to find the smallest space for the water.

WHAT THE JUDGES LOOK FOR

What is it that makes an exhibit a prizewinner? What makes the judge choose one exhibit over all the others in the class? What are the judges looking for? How do they judge? These and many other questions all run through the minds of competitors especially those who are fairly new to show work.

Let us remember that judges are there to help, and are *for* the competitors, not *against* them. You may not always have the opportunity of speaking with the judges at shows but a great deal can be learned from studying the written comment cards that they leave on the exhibits. Particularly helpful are the suggestions they make for improving the design if you can relate them to the exhibits and picture for yourself how they could look. If you do not understand what is meant by the comments, ask the judges themselves as they are usually only too willing to explain. If they are not available, ask a more experienced competitor.

Remember, too, that it is not only the competitors but also the judges who will have studied the schedule, as they will have received a draft copy beforehand to vet for ambiguous wording and any other points likely to cause misunderstanding. If any class requires special research the judges will have done this prior to the show, so that every possible interpretation by the competitors is understood.

When the time comes for the judges to carry out the task of awarding prizes in each class, they will carefully weigh up the merits of one exhibit against another and arrive at their conclusions without bias or prejudice. It is also their duty to give encouragement to nonprizewinners with helpful, constructive remarks, confident that their judgement is backed by sound reasoning which will stand being questioned if necessary.

So what do the judges look for?

Compliance with the schedule

If the show is being judged in accordance with the 7th edition of the NAFAS *Handbook of Schedule Definitions* and your exhibit does not comply with the schedule for any of the following reasons, it will be disqualified:

1 Exceeding the space stated in the schedule.

2 Using artificial plant material unless the schedule states that it is allowed.

3 Including components when the schedule has prohibited their use *or* omitting a component when the schedule has called for its particular use.

4 Using any fresh plant material whose stems are not in water or water-retaining material.

Disqualification can be avoided by repeatedly studying the wording of the schedule, and then checking and re-checking that not one of the above four points applies to your exhibit.

There may be some shows, not judged according to NAFAS rules that do not involve actual disqualification, but obviously the rules and requirements of that particular schedule must be carried out.

Having eliminated any entries which are 'not according to schedule' the judges will adhere to the following principles.

Appropriate interpretation

Although an exhibit must comply with the wording in the schedule, this does not necessarily mean that it interprets the title well. For example, in a class entitled 'Besides Still Waters', the competitor may have used a flat container suitable for an arrangement 'featuring water' and also used moisture-loving plant material in greens, blues and creams, but has then over-filled the container with too many varieties thus creating a dense marsh-like exhibit instead of a cool, serene scene suggested by the title. When the schedule states 'featuring water', approximately two thirds of the water used should be seen, and the plant material kept to a minimum.

Plant material in good condition

Your plant material must be in good condition, undamaged and unblemished. It should be well conditioned (as explained in Ch. 6) to ensure that not only is it not wilting at the time of judging but that it is still perfectly fresh at dismantling time. The plant material must always predominate and should be well chosen for the class. Bear in mind that it is plant material and not your accessories which should convey the message and interpret the title of the class.

Overall design

'Design' means the shape of your exhibit as a whole. Good design incorporates scale and balance. Your exhibit will be judged on good use of design principles: balance, scale, proportion, dominance, contrast, rhythm and harmony.

The judges will take into consideration how your container, plant material, accessories, background and base all relate to each other and to the space allowed for staging. It is the amount of space allowed for your exhibit which will dictate the size of your container, plant material and accessories. Are they in scale with each other?

There are two categories of **balance** – actual and visual. Both are equally important. We can see at once when our plant material is tipping forward, backwards or sideways, and does not appear to be sitting happily in its container after it has been arranged so that it seems about to topple over. This means that its *actual* balance is in jeopardy. *Visual* balance on the other hand is achieved in two ways, either by equally distributing the weight of the plant material on either side of an imaginary central line, or by using colour to give a visual impression of equal weight, in which case we rely on our eyes to tell us when the balance is correct.

Visual balance may be *symmetrical* when each side of the imaginary central line is equal in size, shape and depth of colour. This does not mean that it is necessary to use the identical variety of plant material, stem by stem, on either side, but it does mean you must use the same type of plant material and depth of colour, giving two sides of equal shape, size and weight.

By contrast, visual balance may be *asymmetrical*. If long sprays of, for example, boconnia, jasmin, clematis seed heads and montbretia were used as outline material on one side of the imaginary line, and camelia foliage, aspidistra leaves and gladoli were used on the opposite side, the heavy leaves and blooms of the latter would immediately make the exhibit appear lop-sided and out of balance. To restore the balance, add to the lighter side flowers and foliage which are either bolder in colour or larger in size or proportion than those on the heavy side. If your eye is not drawn to one side more than the other you have obtained visual balance even though your outline is not exactly equal on both sides (figure 18).

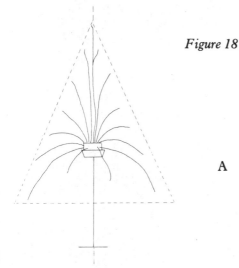

Figure 18

A

1   Symmetrical triangle with outlines equal on both sides forming triangle: balanced

2   Asymmetrical triangle with outline shorter one side than other: not balanced.

2   Addition of weight at centre by use of large leaves. Majority of weight added to left side to start balancing asymmetrical sides: better balance than A 2 but still not balanced.

1   Addition of weight at centre by use of large leaves: balanced

B

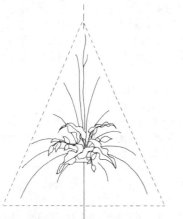

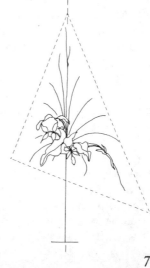

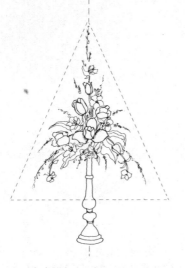

C

1   Addition of similar plant material either side of horizontal axis with focal point in centre of triangle: balanced.

2   Addition of heavier plant material on narrower side to balance lighter plant material on wider: balanced.

An exhibit may appear clumsy and awkward because it looks top heavy. In a traditional exhibit, plant material which is more pointed and lighter in shape and colour should be placed at the top and used to outline your arrangement, while darker, more solid and bolder foliage and flowers should be placed towards the centre. If the darker, more solid plant material is placed at the top of the exhibit, it would appear to be leaning on, or even squashing, the lighter more delicate plant material below.

Judges also take into account the scale and proportion of your exhibit. **Scale** denotes the size of one component as compared with another (each should be neither too large nor too small). **Proportion** denotes the volume of one component as compared with another (one should not overwhelm the rest). The various components – container, plant material, accessories – should be in scale and proportion with each other (figure 19). Thought must be given to the size of:

1 the different kinds of plant material – a forget-me-not would look ridiculous with a hydrangea or paeony

2 the container to the plant material

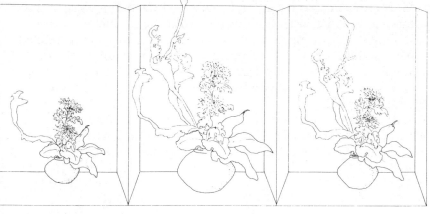

a   b   c

Figure 19   Scale and proportion – filling the space
a)   Too small with container too far back
b)   Too large with plant material over top and touching sides
c)   Correct

3 the accessories to the other components
4 the base to the exhibit
5 the exhibit to the space allowed.

Dominance is another important factor in the design of your exhibit. Some parts of your exhibit should be more important than the rest, otherwise it becomes uninteresting and monotonous. Your plant material must always predominate, but there should be some which attracts more attention, and forms, in a traditional exhibit, your focal point. Dominance can be created by bright shiny colours, shiny texture and size.

The need for **contrast** is as important for the same reasons as the need for dominance. Similar shapes, textures, colours and sizes would produce a most uninteresting exhibit. For traditional exhibits, choose some spiky, plant material, some with shiny and some with dull surfaces, some with feathery leaves and some with bold. For traditional exhibits, variety is perhaps more desirable than contrast, especially in the choice of colour of the plant material. Modern and abstract arrangements, however, rely to a large extent on contrast for impact.

Rhythm is important because it draws the eye from one part of the exhibit to the whole, and then to the focal point. It is rhythm which can create the required atmosphere, giving either a feeling of peace and tranquility, or one of activity or violence.

Harmony, another essential, is achieved by avoiding the use of any components which are out of keeping with the exhibit as a whole. It is achieved by ensuring that all your components are suitably related.

Your exhibit should have originality which should be achieved without gimmicks of any kind and certainly without choosing a theme intended to shock or which would in any way be distasteful to the viewing public.

Distinction is that indefinable something that a judges always look for but do not always find. It is an important quality that lifts one exhibit above the rest, making it an undisputed prizewinner.

8. Group Exhibits

Whether the group exhibits are for competition or exhibition in stately homes, cathedrals or churches, the formula is the same.

Before considering the actual exhibit, first concentrate on your 'group'. Unless the number is stipulated in the schedule this can be any number of people. Beware! There is a great deal of truth in the old proverb 'too many cooks spoil the broth'. Place your own restrictions on the numbers actually staging the exhibit. Two, or, at the most, three are usually sufficient for a really large space. More may be involved in the planning but not in the execution.

The members of the group should be picked with care. You need to consider not only their flower arranging ability, but the likelihood that they will work together happily and enjoy it. They need to 'jell' otherwise, strange though it may sound, it shows in the finished exhibit. Seldom do you find a club or association having a permanent 'group exhibit team'. So the chances of the arrangers in the team having had the experience of working together previously are slight. But everybody who has the ability and inclination should be given the opportunity to help stage a large exhibit, even though the fact that the space allowed is larger than anything they have previously tackled might make them feel apprehensive at first, this will pass as the planning and involvement progresses.

PICKING THE TEAM

'Team' means a group of people working together, and this is just what they must do – work and arrange together. There are people who are excellent flower arrangers but at the same time are individualists. Unfortunately you must forget all about them when selecting the team. They would not be a happy choice and could ruin the exhibit as well as the enjoyment of the rest of the group. Each member must be able to work as part of a team – you cannot have individualists in a group exhibit otherwise it ends up looking like three or four unrelated exhibits.

One of the team must be appointed the leader. She should not only be a good flower arranger but have imagination, tact, a capacity for hard work and be a perfectionist. The others in the group should be quite prepared to accept her authority, because it is the finished exhibit which counts, not each individual placement.

A less experienced member can be brought in as the 'go for girl' – going for this and going for that, unloading materials, filling buckets, parking the car, soaking your plant material and water-retaining foam, and dispensing coffee. This experience is a great help to her, and her help is a great benefit to you. Remember to include her when you have your mock-up.

SCOPE OF GROUP EXHIBITS

Group exhibits may be any size and any shape, from 3 ft (91 cm.) diameter circle to as much as a 10 ft (3 m.) run of tabling. They may be raised 8 or 9 in. (20 cm. or 22 cm.) from the ground, or be at table height i.e., 2 ft 6 in. (75 cm.). More space than you have been called upon to fill before, perhaps, but do not make it even larger by exceeding the space allocated in the schedule. This is a common fault with group exhibits, and it is upsetting both for the judges and competitors alike because it does mean disqualification at the majority of shows, and what might have been a prizewinner cannot be considered at all because of that additional inch or so. You may be given unrestricted height. What a joy. Use it.

Not all competitive shows have the space for very large exhibits, but throughout the country many stately homes, cathedrals and churches are mounting Festivals of Flowers where the larger exhibits almost outnumber the small ones. Visit as many of these as you can, including the flower arranging tent at the Royal Horticultural Society's Spring Show at Chelsea.

Whilst looking at the many good qualities of the large exhibits, make notes of any weaknesses and faults, and decide how you can avoid making the same mistakes. A great deal can be learned by studying how the windows are dressed in the larger shops and stores. Notice where the centre of interest is placed; how the accessories are cleverly grouped to direct your eye to the main product and enhance it. Study, too, the way the fabric is draped so that it links to make a whole; the use of texture; how space is allocated. Note how overcrowding is avoided in the same way that it should be with flowers and accessories, not too full and not too empty, so that the available space is both clean and uncluttered.

Do not be misled into thinking that because you have been given more space than your normal 2 ft 6 in. (75 cm.) or 3 ft (91 cm.), you can now put everything but the kitchen sink into your exhibit. As with individual exhibits, it is your plant material which should predominate over all the other components, and bring the class title to life by the clever choice of plant material. It is your plant material which is the basis of your exhibit, not drapes and accessories. These, too, can play their part but it should be a minor, yet harmonizing one. As always, your accessories should be chosen with great care; their proportion, their shape and colour all being of equal importance. They should, moreover be in scale with other components and your plant material. They play a supporting role, and well supported they must be. Because they are probably larger than those used in an individual exhibit, and because you may, if the staging is raised from the floor, need to stand on it after your accessories are in place, they do need to be very firmly fixed.

PLANNING YOUR EXHIBITS

When you set about planning and staging the exhibit carefully check your schedule so that you know the exact amount of space you have been given, the type of staging, the colour on and against which the exhibit is to be staged, and any restrictions such as the use of artificial plant material. If you are not certain whether you can use paper or silk flowers, find out. Ask the competition secretary. This is a case of the old saying 'if in doubt leave out' being altered to 'if in doubt find out'.

Whether you are working for a competition or an exhibition, the need for research into your class title or subject is of paramount importance and should be undertaken by all members of the team, each listing their findings and ideas before you decide on a theme. Pooling ideas and suggestions can produce an exhibit with both originality and distinction. Although you must take into account the space allocated, this will hopefully be restricted in width and depth only, allowing you to produce as tall an exhibit as good scaling will allow.

Make use of your stands, plinths, boxes and tins, carefully covered or concealed by a drape, to achieve added interest and elegance by varying the heights of your exhibits. Varying the size and height of each exhibit is essential. The eyes need to be drawn upwards, as well as round and across. An extra inch or centimetre may be added to the height of your exhibit provided it is in scale, but never, never, go beyond the width or depth allotted, unless you are producing a table decoration. This is, however, an unlikely subject for a group to be given.

As well as being led upwards your eyes need to have a focal point on which to rest, therefore one of the placements should be more dominant than the rest. All the others should lead into and away from it. The interest should be carried from one well linked placement to the next by good use of colour and plant material. But there should be enough space to prevent them all merging together and losing their independent beauty. The focal point, or centre of interest, may be anywhere in the exhibit provided its balance is retained. The balance is more difficult to achieve when the focal point is 'off centre' and seen from all sides, but a more pleasing and interesting exhibit may result. A large-scale exhibit prepared by more than one person must still follow the basic principles of design, incorporating balance, scale, proportion, dominance, contrast and rhythm. It is proportion which can so easily go wrong, and, unfortunately, frequently does when large exhibits are staged. All the components may be in scale, the plant material with the containers, the accessories with the plant material, but often the end product is crowded and 'there is no room for the butterflies'. This is because the plant material has been used in profusion instead of with restraint.

Decide on your theme which should not be too restrictive but should produce many ideas from which to choose. Dismiss the obvious interpretation and decide instead on the one which is not quite so evident but more original. Make it one which can be easily interpreted by your plant material rather than by your accessories. Make certain that it conforms with the stipulations in the schedule, and then arrange a 'mock-up'.

THE ESSENTIAL 'MOCK-UP'

A 'mock-up' is essential however experienced you are. It will enable you to assemble all possible containers, accessories, drapes and backgrounds which may be needed. Decide on the style of your exhibits and the plant material required. For the mock-up or run through, there is no necessity to buy expensive flowers or pick precious foliage, but substitute plant material of a similar shape, form and colour. This will be perfectly adequate for finding out whether you are on the right road. In any case, there is no necessity to buy expensive flowers for the show or exhibition itself, unless the class specifically calls for the more unusual or exotic florist flowers such as anthuriums, gerberas, strelitzia or orchids. What is necessary is to have plant material of suitable colour, shape and texture for your theme. It should also be in perfect condition, having been treated correctly before staging.

STAGING YOUR 'MOCK-UP'

If your exhibit is to be staged on a raised base, then do stage your mock-up on a base which has been raised to the same height. It is surprising how different the whole arrangement will look when staged at the show or exhibition if you have planned it all at ground level. Whether it is to be on individual platforms or tabling, measure out the exact width, depth and height if this is restricted. If the schedule states you are to be given a coloured fabric background, try to stage your mock-up against a wall. Nail up an old sheet or tablecloth as near the stated colour as possible, even if it means dying it the correct colour. If no clear wall space is available, make a background frame by using two uprights and a cross bar, or by sinking pieces of dowel, thick bamboo or cane cut to the required height into large coffee jars of wet cement, and allowing it to set. You will, of course require two of these. Place a piece of dowel, bamboo or cane the same length as the width of your exhibit across the top. This can be resting on nails or cup hooks. Throw your old sheet, tablecloth or even disused club staging material over the top, or attach it with drawing pins. This does not take much time to assemble and is worth every minute spent on it, because it is vital to have your 'stage' accurately measured if your mock-up is to be worthwhile. 'Near enough' is not good enough – it must be correct.

You will be extremely fortunate if the perfect exhibit can be planned at one meeting; a second or even a third is usually necessary. When you feel satisfied that your containers and accessories are all in the best possible position, and nothing will overlap the allotted space, this is the time to put your plan on to a piece of graph paper, marking where and how you have placed these vital components. You may also find it helpful if using driftwood to mark the wood itself in some way, denoting which way round you have decided to place it. How often have we used several pieces together giving us enormous satisfaction, but have had the utmost difficulty assembling them quite so well the next time. Marking it saves much time and frustration when it comes to the actual staging, and starts you off in a relaxed manner, rather than all tensed up because the 'props' are not right.

Stand back and assess your exhibit from the same position as the judges and viewing public will be seeing it. Is it a good interpretation of the class title? Has it interest and originality and that elusive distinction? Is it balanced? Has the interest been carried through and is there something to hold the attention of the viewer from wherever they may be standing? Does one exhibit lead your eye into the next? Satisfied? If not, start again now. It will be too late at the show.

PREPARING YOUR ARRANGEMENT

List everything you are using and will need to take with you. Make one list, with copies for each member of the team, marking who is responsible for bringing each item. This way you can see when everything has an initial by it denoting that it is somebody's responsibility. This may appear to be too obvious to mention, but it has been known for something to be left behind because each thought the other was bringing it. Now all you need is a smooth journey to the show so that you arrive in good time to stage your interesting exhibit. Enjoy every moment.

Packing and transporting plant material for individual exhibits has been dealt with on pages 71-3. For group exhibits the method is the same, but the journey may be longer and size of the plant material larger. The same amount of care is required for each. A few extra pieces of plant material should be included as replacements if the show lasts a long time, or if they get damaged. They should be too well conditioned to wilt. Do not take too many extra pieces, just a few then there is not the temptation to use it because you have brought it. Remember your exhibit must be in proportion.

STAGING YOUR EXHIBIT

On arrival at the show and before unpacking anything, find your space, then unload. If working space is limited, it is sometimes advisable to unpack your drapes, background, containers and accessories, leaving your plant material in its boxes and buckets. But make sure it is not left in the car in the sun. This is not the time for a reunion with old friends. That can come later when both you and they will be more relaxed and have time to enjoy a gossip.

Your mechanics need fixing firmly into your containers. Remember to leave space if using water-retaining foam to enable sufficient water to be added. Then take out your plan, and put up the drapes and background, placing them exactly how and where you decided at the final mock-up. Do not change your mind now or confusion will reign. Care should be taken with these first placements. If they are in the wrong positions, whether they are accessories or containers, then the subsequent ones will be affected too, and before you know it your balance will have gone, or your spacing will be incorrect.

When you are quite satisfied your drapes, background and containers are exactly where they should be, take the precaution of covering your base, tabling or drapes around the containers with plastic sheeting to protect them from being marked by water spillage or plant material. By this time your plant material from the boxes should have been put in buckets, the ends of the stems recut on the slant. This should be done by one of the team who is not coping with the drapes, etc.

You are now ready to start arranging. Allow yourself time at the end to stand back and assess the exhibit. Take a break, walk away, you will be surprised how different it will appear when you come back to it. Make sure your containers are filled, and do not forget any cones and tubes. Spray well, but first protect the drapes. Clear all rubbish. Take it home with you rather than leaving it lying around – after all you did bring it! Check that your exhibitor's class card is there, and that your title card is standing firmly and can be easily seen and read.

You have done your part, and now it is time for the judges to do theirs. If you do not receive an award, you may feel disappointed because you have followed all the rules and tried hard. But it has been fun, and there is always next time. You have been a vital part of the show and cannot fail to find new friends and benefit in so many ways.

9. Festivals of Flowers

Apart from competitive shows, we are privileged to play a small part in exhibitions of another kind. These are festivals of flowers staged throughout the country in many stately homes, cathedrals, abbeys and churches, enjoyed by visitors and local people alike. Taking part in these festivals can be our way of making a contribution to the community, whether we are 'old hands' or 'newcomers' to flower arranging. It is a token of appreciation for all the pleasure we derive from our flower arranging. In spite of the hustle and bustle on staging day, there is a sense of peace, enjoyment and goodwill.

It is a great privilege to work in buildings of such architectural beauty and splendour, and, but for our flowers, such an opportunity might not have come our way. In which case we would have missed not just seeing, but working amongst the splendid sculptures and other beautiful works of art. This is why we must be very careful that this privilege is not abused. Flower arrangers, have, over the years, built up a reputation of caring, not only for the plant material on display but for the buildings in which it is exhibited, and leaving them as clean and tidy as when we arrived. We must continue to do this because these buildings are our heritage, and we should be there because we care about their preservation and embellishment. By raising funds for a new church roof, repairing the organ or supporting a particular charity, we can go on giving pleasure and help to others through our flowers, while we, in turn, have the joy of 'doing the flowers' in places of such beauty.

PLANNING THE FESTIVAL

In planning a festival, be it in a stately home, cathedral or village church, one thought should be uppermost in our minds – consideration for the 'inhabitants'. The owners of the stately home or the incumbents of the church should be consulted throughout on all aspects of the festival. It is most important to show them your proposed design, to indicate where you would like to stage the arrangements and to obtain their permission before any details are discussed with the arrangers. Your plan may need to be altered.

Another point, which is applicable in all cases regardless of venue, is restraint. Difficult sometimes when you have so many good ideas, but flowers must enhance and not obscure. Neither stately homes nor churches should be over decorated so that there is too little space both for the viewing public and for the actual arrangements themselves.

Festivals do not just happen, they must be carefully planned many months ahead. For this a committee needs to be formed once the date and the length of the festival has been established. The activities of the committee are similar for stately homes, cathedrals or churches, and therefore the following suggestions can be adapted according to the size and type of building, which will obviously dictate the size and scope of the festival.

COMMITTEE ACTIVITIES

The chairman is responsible for the overall organization of the festival. It is helpful if she is also one of the designers. She should make sure that the wishes of the owners or incumbents of the building concerned are considered at all times, and that the plans are fully discussed with them. A good relationship between them and the festival organizers is essential. If a church is the venue it is often advantageous to invite either the Vicar or a member of the parochial church council to one or more committee meeting, especially if a festival of flowers has never been staged in that church before. It enables queries to be answered on the spot, and gives the church authorities an insight into how much detailed planning and organization is undertaken by the flower arrangers. If we expect to receive co-operation we must be prepared to give it so that a happy atmosphere and sense of well being prevails from the start.

The following points should be discussed and mutually agreed at the outset: the date and length of the festival; its theme or title; the opening and closing times of the festival itself, and the times at which the flower arranging may be done; festival finances: including allowances for flowers, staging, printing, extra insurance (if needed for accident and theft), publicity, road signs (by the AA or RAC) and catering costs; staging day requirements such as the availability of water and disposal of rubbish; and the possible involvement of stately home staff, church members or charity helpers throughout the festival with stewarding and other duties.

It is wise to have agreement on these details in writing so that nobody is in any doubt about them, and difficulties and misunderstandings which could occur later are avoided.

FINANCIAL MATTERS

Whatever size the festival may be, money will be involved. One person who is appointed treasurer should be responsible for this throughout. A bank account should be opened, and two people nominated to sign cheques on behalf of the festival committee. Night-safe facilities during the festival should be arranged. A simple budget should be prepared after the festival theme and plans have been approved. This should allow for: flowers and staging; arrangers' and committee expenses, e.g., travel, postage and telephone calls; publicity; printing; and extra insurance.

These expenses will of course be offset by certain income, from admission charges; collections; donations; and fund-raising events. At this stage such income can only be estimated. Agreement should be reached before the festival whether the responsibility for emptying the collecting plates, boxes and jars at the end of each day falls on the festival treasurer or a member of the church.

THE NEED FOR PUBLICITY

Without good publicity the whole event can be a waste of time, talent, energy and money resulting in bitter disappointment for all concerned. Anything which is happening at the local stately home, cathedral or church is news and will attract a certain amount of attention in the immediate area, but for a festival with all the planning and organization which it entails, the news must be spread far and wide. The amount allowed for publicity must be budgeted for and be a joint venture between the flower arrangers and the stately home, cathedral or church concerned, all working together.

Think big – this is an event not to be missed so round up all the help you can early on. Whet people's appetites with a good press release as soon as you have some firm details. Follow this up at regular intervals with releases to the local press, the national press, the British Tourist Authority, the English Tourist Board (which requires details at least one year ahead). Nearer the event, insert an advertisement or submit a story featuring a local clergyman or a member of his congregation, a member of the flower club, or a characteristic of the stately home, church or charity involved, in the most appropriate of the following publications: *Church Times*, *Catholic Herald, The Methodist Recorder*, the local parish magazine, the countryside magazine for that area, gardening or flower arranging magazines and journals, the local and national press, and local and national radio and TV.

Circulate handbills to the local Women's Institute and Townswomen's Guild, to neighbouring flower clubs, to the local library, hotels and shops who will all usually publicize the event if you give them a handbill each, attractively displayed on a piece of card with perhaps an edging or corner of dried flowers. This will create far more impact than a notice stuck on the 'What's On' board in a hotel or on the window of your local newsagent's shop. Enlist the help of the Boy Scouts and Girl Guides to deliver handbills locally. Ask the information bureau in the area to take some handbills to advertise the event.

Banners, which must be well presented, placed along the railings of the church or hoisted across the road are eye-catching. It is advisable to check with the local authority that you are allowed to hang a banner across the road. It would obviously need to be high up and well clear of the tops of buses and lorries. Sailmakers or sometimes prisons can be a source of supply.

Car stickers can be used in many other places as well as cars. Shops sometimes prefer these to handbills or posters as they are smaller and take up less space in their windows. Local people might display them in their front windows.

If you are planning to use AA or RAC directorial signs, they need to be booked at least six months before the festival. These signs are excellent publicity in themselves, as well as serving the purpose for which they are intended.

A press preview is a must, even for the smallest festival. Reporter's like to see things happening so invite them as early as possible on staging day to enable them to catch the same evening's edition of their newspaper. This will mean having at least one of the arrangements finished early. A write-up and photograph prior to or during the festival is far more helpful than anything which appears afterwards. Refreshments should be offered and a press release made available.

When you hold your preview this should if possible be covered by a reporter and certainly by a photographer. They need to work in close liaison with the owners of the stately home or with the clergy of the church concerned. Permission should be obtained before booking the services of a professional photographer, if you are thinking of having a set of slides. Invariably permission is granted, but in some cases for security reasons only certain parts of a building are allowed to be photographed. When this is the case, press passes should be issued to all those invited to attend the press preview and other functions.

GUIDANCE ON PRINTING

This may not be the responsibility of the flower-arranging committee if the owners of the building where the festival is to be held regularly use their own printers, but they may need guidance as to requirements. If the printing involved is the responsibility of the committee, more than one estimate of the cost should be obtained, and a first proof of all the work carried out should be asked for.

Handbills are the first priority as these act as an advance press release. They should include the title of the festival, its venue and the dates and times of opening, any special features, car parking and refreshments facilities, and the name and address of the person to contact for further information.

Other items which need to be printed are posters, car stickers, tickets for any ancillary events such as the preview or special service, and a list of flower arrangers if not included in the brochure.

A good calligrapher is a wonderful asset for producing quotations or title cards to place with the arrangements. Additional notices and arrows marking the exits and the route, requesting 'please do not touch', and marking the whereabouts may also be required. These should be clear, well written and displayed above head level.

If you are producing a commemorative brochure, close co-operation between the flower arrangers and the owners of the venue is essential. It should be very much a combined effort, and include such items as a message from the owner of the stately home or from the dean or other clergy; a brief history of the venue; a plan marking the route and position of the flower arrangements; a list of the arrangements with the arrangers' names; information about the flower club; and what the profit from the festival is to be used for. There should also be acknowledgement of any special assistance received.

STEWARDING

This should also be a joint undertaking. Your stately home may, if it is normally open to the public, have a certain number of regular stewards who will be well versed in the history of the house. With a church or cathedral the friends of the cathedral and church workers will most certainly enjoy being involved in the stewarding of the festival. A rota should be carefully worked out so that everybody knows when they are on duty and where; whether they are expected to sell brochures; what the exact route is so they can make sure it is adhered to; and the position of the cloakroom. Whilst on duty they must make certain that the flower arrangements and precious objects are not touched.

On staging and dismantling day a band of willing helpers will be required to assist with unloading; supply large bags for rubbish; and provide additional water in dustbins if the supply is inadequate.

The committee member in charge of organizing the stewards should provide easily recognizable sashes or badges for them to wear; see that route signs and arrows are in place and be prepared to redirect the flow of traffic if bottlenecks occur; and draw up a rota of people to water, 'top-up', and spray the flower arrangements.

Unless somebody else has the job of organizing helpers for the car parking area (this could be undertaken by the local Boy Scouts or members of the church choir), provision for this will be necessary. Car badges for the helpers and special visitors will also be needed. The police should be given due notification about the festival at least one month in advance, followed by a written reminder the week before the event.

CATERING ARRANGEMENTS

Catering is another job which may not be part of the flower-arrangers' committee duties. The Women's Institute or Mother's Union might like to tackle this. But the Chairman should discuss the catering requirements for the festival with the people concerned and decide whether and when refreshment will be served, by whom and how much they are to cost. If a flower club undertakes the catering, the area where refreshments are to be served will need to be seen in advance, and the availability of china, cutlery, tablecloths, trays, tables, chairs and kitchen facilities noted. You will also need a rota of helpers to order, prepare and dispose of (surplus) food.

THE DESIGNER'S RESPONSIBILITIES

Nothing has yet been said about the all-important designer's role and this is because it leads naturally to the design and type of arrangements, but there are certain committee jobs and responsiblities to be undertaken by the designer apart from the artistic planning, which will be discussed later.

The designer is responsible for submitting her preliminary plan to the owners of the stately home or to the church authorities, obtaining permission at this stage for the movement of any furniture, the removal of any valuable articles to a safe place, the placing of any arrangements on tables or other furniture, the use of church treasures, plate or vestments, the provision of additional lighting or spot lighting for dark corners or for special arrangements, the use of stepladders, and for arranging storage space for replacement plant material.

The arrangers will want to know as early as possible what they are expected to do, especially if they need to do any research. The following details should be sent to them: their position in the building, the colour, style and shape and measurements of their flower arrangement; suggested plant material, container and mechanics; the theme or interpretation (if any); whether refreshments are available on staging day; date and time they may view their position; and the staging and dismantling times.

There should be a note at the bottom of the form stressing the importance of using polythene sheeting to protect floors and furniture from water spillage. If it is possible to include a floor plan with the flower arranger's position marked, it is extremely helpful.

Flowers and foliage may be donated from nurseries or be given by members of the congregation, and these will need conditioning and distributing on staging day to the arrangers. It is always advisable to have spare staging mechanics such as watering cans, sprays, polythene sheeting, tubes and cones, and water-retaining foam.

DESIGNING FOR A STATELY HOME

If possible the designer should make more than one visit to the stately home, should read the guide book, and, if necessary do additional research before beginning to design. Consideration must be given to what is already there, the aim being at all times to complement rather than to conceal the decorative features and precious possessions. The design should be restrained rather than over-flowing into every nook and cranny. The age of the building, the setting and the furnishing in each room will dictate the colour of the plant material and also the style which is invariably traditional. Paintings and portraits may be emphasized or complemented.

This may be one of the few occasions when an arrangement can be reflected in a mirror, so that care must be taken to make the back as good as the front, and to conceal carefully all mechanics. Fireplaces and their surrounds may be beautiful but the actual grate is rarely attractive, and your immediate reaction may be to use this space and put a beautiful arrangement there. Before you do, find out whether the chimney has been filled in. If it has not, then the idea is best forgotten because the inevitable draught will be death to your plant material. There is also the possibility of the arrangement being hidden by people standing in front of it. Another place where draughts are likely is the entrance hall, and all arrangements staged near the door must be very securely anchored. A welcoming colour should be chosen because this is the first impression visitors will have. From the entrance hall a one-way traffic system is essential, and private rooms should be clearly marked 'No admission', and visitors kept out by ropes and stands if necessary.

PREPARING A CHURCH FESTIVAL

One of the most important points to keep uppermost in your mind is a sense of scale. Because of the size and height of the building practically everything will need to be larger than usual – bigger arrangements requiring larger flowers and foliage with longer stems. Although the arrangements must be large that does not mean a great many are required. There should be space both in and around the arrangements. Restraint should still be the key word, and the flowers should complement in colour and style the natural beauty of the fabric of the church – the stone, the wood, the marble, the stained-glass windows and any special historical features, so that both church and flowers are admired together. Make the most of the beautiful feature and minimize an unsightly one by positioning an eye-catching arrangement just beyond it.

Churches are frequently dark, and rely on artificial light all the year round. Colours therefore need to be bright. Cream, apricot, yellow, orange, pink and orange/red are good for dimly-lit areas, and blues, mauves and blue/reds where the light is good, otherwise they are inclined to disappear. If you are able to have additional lights in dark corners, or spotlights to highlight a particular arrangement, do not place them too near the flowers because the heat will dry the atmosphere round them and they will wilt very quickly.

Other points to be considered are the area where the sun is the strongest; where the radiators are placed if the festival is staged in the winter; the lighting which will be needed in summer and winter; if sockets are available for extra lighting; the positions of monuments and wall plaques; what can be seen when the congregation stand during a service; the placing of arrangements where they do not hinder the clergy in their duties, interfere with the functional use of the choir stalls, or obstruct the view of the congregation.

The theme or title of the festival should have been agreed at the very outset and the design based on it should observe ecclesiastical rules and be approved by the clergy. Some popular themes are: a history of the church or village; the life of the saint to whom the church is dedicated; texts from the Bible; and verses from hymns. Although several of these, especially the last two, have been used over and over again, the interpretations have varied enormously.

Certain colours are used to celebrate the festivals of the Church throughout the year, and most churches use these colours for their altar frontals and vestments:

Advent	Blue or violet	Whitsun	Red
	(sometimes no flowers)	Trinity	Gold and green
Epiphany	Green; sometimes white/gold	All Saints	White and red
Easter	White predominating over gold	Christmas	White and gold

Therefore, when planning your colour scheme take into consideration the colour of the altar frontal and vestments. Ask to see the ones which will be in use at the time of the festival. Take notice of the colour of the carpet, hymn book covers, kneelers and choir robes. When considering the stained-glass windows do not be tempted to pick out all the colours, concentrate on one, or, at the most, two. Vestments do look superb on raised plinths with the flowers harmonizing in colour and style with them.

At an early stage the responsibilities of the cathedral staff and the flower arrangers must be defined as this saves misunderstanding later. The following points should be discussed: whether the cathedral is to be closed to the public on staging day as it is much easier if flower arrangers have the building to themselves; whether there will be a cold room for storage of plant material required for replacements; whether extra ladders or even a gantry will be available if required, and whether trolleys can be borrowed from the supermarkets to wheel the arrangers' materials around; and whether a room will be available for the organizing committee. Unloading, on both staging and dismantling days is likely to cause traffic problems, so the local police should be alerted and asked to help. Festivals of flowers are costly affairs, so it must be decided whether sponsorship should be sought and, if so, from whom and by whom. If sponsors are involved they should be sent a complimentary ticket to the preview and acknowledged in the brochure.

If an admission fee is being charged and tickets sold in advance, there should be two entrance doors, so that those who have already paid do not join the queue for the cash desk. Arrangers and helpers should be provided with passes enabling them to pass in and out when the occasion demands. It must also be decided whether there will be a reduction in price for children under a certain age, and adults over a certain age.

In order to preserve a happy relationship between the flower arrangers and church helpers, such as the flower rota ladies who decorate the many churches throughout the land every week, do not walk into their church and ignore them but invite them to participate so that all can work together for a single purpose – the glory of God. There is something for everybody to do. The less skilled can be shown how to make garlands and kneelers, while research and interpretations of the monuments, windows and plaques can be carried out by those who have had more practice.

The plant material should be used to interpret the theme rather than the accessories, and even drapes should be kept to a minimum, to avoid hiding the attractive stone and wood which are ideal backgrounds for the flowers and foliage. Gimmickry should be avoided at all times.

The style of the church will dictate the style of your arrangements, which will need to be placed higher than usual, using swags, plaques, garlands and cone, none of which are difficult to make.

FESTIVALS IN CATHEDRALS

All that has been written about mounting a festival in a church applies with a few additional suggestions to a cathedral. The following points may be useful for designers. Before you embark on the design make several visits to the cathedral and do your research thoroughly. Buy the official guide which will give you the chronology and building history. Read carefully. Ideas will come to mind. A further visit with guide book and notepad in hand and you will be getting the 'feeling' of the cathedral, and suddenly the theme will come to you. By now you will realize that the cathedral cannot be viewed as a whole, and your designs must be in areas which are seen together, and then co-ordinated into a whole. Everywhere you must think tall as the size of the building dwarfs all flower arrangements. If you are able to use the cloisters, these will give the space and opportunity for staging large interpretative arrangements. You may also be allowed to use some of the lovely vestments and copes. Do treat them with loving care, and choose arrangers who will do the same.

The flower arrangers' committee and cathedral staff should prepare a list of people who have helped and insert it into the brochure. Free admission or preview tickets may also be given as a token of appreciation. It should be decided whether advertisements will be included in the brochure, and if so, the rates to be charged should be agreed.

10. A Different Kind of Arranging

Normally we arrange our plant material in containers which hold water or water-retaining foam, but in cathedrals and churches, where some flowers need to be raised to greater heights than usual so that they can be seen, swags, plaques and garlands are very effective, and fun to do. Both fresh and preserved plant material may be used, making for variety in the plant material as well as in the style of arrangements.

SWAGS

The ideal way of hanging a swag is from a nail or screw, and with careful scrutiny existing ones may be found in church walls and pillars, but if not, permission to knock in nails must be sought. However, if knocking in nails is not allowed, nylon fishing line tied firmly round a pillar or to the pulpit or screen can be used. Fresh or preserved plant material can be used to cover up the mechanics and backing.

If you use fresh plant material keep your water-retaining foam to a minimum to reduce its weight when it is wet. Remember that a large swag can be made from a fairly small block by using long-stemmed plants. Tie pieces of soaked foam of the required size on to peg- board of the same size, having first wrapped them in thin polythene. Use tape or string for this rather than wire, as these do not cut into the foam. Make a loop for hanging by threading wire through the holes near the top. Insert your plant material into the foam through the polythene. A skewer or old knitting needle is useful for making holes if the stems are thin or fragile. Cover the foam with shrubby foliage and leaves, hiding the mechanics before inserting your longer stems of differing lengths, recessing some to avoid a stuffed-cushion appearance.

Employ the same method for dried plant material as for fresh, using dry foam instead of wet, or omitting the foam and wiring the stems through the holes. Plant material such as seed heads, fruit, nuts and cones can be mounted on 22-gauge wire and then glued to the peg board or to the heavier plant material. An alternative method for dried plant material is to use crumpled newspaper rolled into the desired shape and covered with 1 in. (2.5 cm.) mesh wire netting. Insert the stems between the wire and the newspaper. The heavier stems will require mounting on wires. Swags may be used on the pulpit, at the end of pews, suspended from a balcony rail or against walls and pillars.

PLAQUES

Plaques are arranged in a similar way to swags, but differ as the backgrounds on which they are arranged are part of the arrangement and visible. The background may be cut to any shape, in hardboard or pegboard, and painted with emulsion paint, covered with suitable fabric such as felt or hessian, or made to look like marble by using Fablon.

When using fresh plant material wrap a piece of water-retaining foam first in thin polythene and then in 1 in. (2.5 cm.) mesh wire netting. Make holes in the hardboard and tie at the back with tape. Cover the mechanics with foliage before inserting the longer stemmed plant material which should not extend over the edge of the backing. The above method may also be applied to dried plant material using dry foam instead of wet, and omitting the polythene.

A more permanent plaque can be made using Daz or modelling clay and attaching it to the board with two long 18-gauge stub wires and wiring through to the back. Insert one north to south over the Daz or clay and take through to the back, and insert the other east to west. Have all your plant material to hand as the clay will set in approximately one hour. Alternatively, dried and preserved plant material may be glued on to the background using UHU or Pritt, but this is inclined to look flat unless more plant material is glued on top.

GARLANDS

Garlands have many uses and can be made in a variety of ways using all types of plant material. They are particularly suitable for pillars, statues, pulpits and fonts, and look most attractive using foliage in different shades of green on its own. Flowers may be placed at intervals in which case it is more effective if one type of flower is used rather than a variety. If a fresh flower arrangement is to be placed in one position only, such as the central point as it hangs down, the position should be marked by winding a piece of wire round the mechanics before commencing to 'green', enabling you to reverse the direction of the foliage when the position of the flowers is reached.

Garlands of fresh plant material can be made as much as ten days ahead if left outside in the shade and sprayed daily. The flowers can then be added when the garland is positioned. An all-foliage garland can be made by binding with 32-gauge reel wire a variety of long-lasting green foliages such as cupressus (variety of shades and types), yew, thuya and box, on to a plastic-coated washing line. Attach your binding wire firmly to one end and, using pieces no longer than 4 in. (10 cm.) (longer pieces do not lay flat when curved round a pillar or statue, and break through the outline), bind these to the rope, bringing your wire down as you work, pulling it taut and covering the previous stem by the next sprig, making sure all foliage goes in the same direction. Fasten off securely when the other end is reached.

When flowers are to be inserted into a garland, water-retaining foam or sphagnum moss will be required where these are to be placed. Use a length of polythene tubing, and insert into it blocks of soaked water-retaining foam, leaving gaps approximately 4 in. (10 cm.) between each to keep the tubing flexible. Twist reel wire round the centre of each gap. Both ends of the tubing should be securely tied with wire leaving an end as a means of fixing. Cover the tube on three sides with foliage. The fourth side will be against the pillar or statue. This is called 'greening'. Green the garland before hanging, popping in odd pieces of foliage to cover any gaps when hung. Flowers or fruit may now be inserted into the foam parcels, the fruit being given false legs or mounted on 18- or 20-gauge wire, according to its weight.

An alternative garland foundation which is not quite so flexible but has its uses and is cheaper, is made from 1 in. (2.5 cm.) mesh wire netting cut to the required length and made into a roll of whatever diameter is needed, or fashioned into the required shape. It is joined together by twisting the cut ends round each other. This should be lined with thin polythene before being filled with sphagnum moss which may be purchased from any florist or garden centre, or may even be raked up from your lawn. Before using the moss, it should be 'teased' apart, taking out any pieces of wood or foreign matter. It can then be pushed into the wire fairly firmly so that it will hold the stems, but not so tightly that you are unable to insert them. If the moss feels dry, spray well after teasing and before inserting.

CONES

Cones can be any size and are an alternative to a vertical arrangement when there is a narrow space to be filled and something tall and slim is required. Cut 1 in. (2.5 cm.) mesh wire netting the desired height or slightly smaller, bearing in mind that the cone will be considerably larger when the plant material has been inserted. To obtain the desired height it is best to draw a paper pattern. Attach a piece of string the length of which is equal to the height of your cone, and draw the arc of a circle. Cut out the pattern, then overlap the two sides until you have the required diameter at the base. Cut off any surplus overlap, then, using your pattern, cut out your wire netting, twisting the cut ends together to join up. Fill with sphagnum moss or old soaked foam, place on a board or plate to prevent the filling from falling out, and stand on an urn-shaped container, or one with a stem. This gives a lighter effect than when placed flat on to your surface. Insert foliage such as box, yew or cupresses to cover the mechanics, coming down *slightly* over the edge, before adding your flowers, fruit or fir cones. Spray well.

HASSOCKS

Fortunately seed boxes are approximately the same size as a hassock so they make a convenient container for a block of water retaining-foam which has been cut into three. Line the bottom of the box with thin polythene sheeting before inserting the foam, leaving sufficient polythene to bring up and over the top. Work out a pattern for your plant material (perhaps based on one being used in the church). The plant stems will all need to be short. Overlapping leaves pinned to the foam by inserting a short piece of 24-gauge stub wire bent into a hairpin near the base of each leaf with the next one overlapping and covering the wire, makes an attractive edging. When completed, the sides of the seed box may be disguised by covering with a band of ribbon, velvet for preference.

HANGING BASKET

Hanging arrangements can look extremely pretty when suspended from beams or hung in a church porch if they are kept light in appearance and do not look like an apple dumpling about to drop on the head of the next visitor. They may be arranged in hanging baskets (as used in the garden), in plastic salad shakers, in balls of sphagnum moss, or in blocks of water-retaining foam covered with thin polythene and then 1 in. (2.5 cm.) mesh wire netting and suspended by a length of nylon fishing line. If using a basket or salad shaker, put a small block of soaked foam covered in polythene and wire netting in the bottom, wiring it to the sides of the basket. It is best to suspend the ball or basket whilst it is being assembled, defining the measurement by inserting a straight-stemmed flower north, south, east and west, and taking your outline from these points. Covering the mechanics by recessing some flowers as well as foliage, to avoid a heavy over-stuffed look, with flower heads all at one level. Allow some of your plant material such as ivy, vinca or honeysuckle to trail down. Hanging baskets will of course be seen from all angles.

TOPIARY TREES

Into a flower pot filled with stones and cement set a broom handle or a 3 ft. 6 in. (97 cm.) length of thick bamboo. Carpets are sometimes delivered on these bamboo lengths, so ask at your local carpet shop. Approximately 1 in. (2.5 cm.) from the top drill holes right through at right angles to each other, one slightly lower than the other. Insert two pieces of wood, 3 in. (7.6 cm.) long, forming four bars on which a block of soaked foam or moss can rest after it has been wrapped in polythene and covered with wire netting. For extra security, bind to the stem with reel wire. Arrange pieces of foliage about 6 in. (15 cm.) long, making them into a light ball with some foliage trailing down. Insert flowers and, if desired, a ribbon bow. The handle of the broom stick should be painted and the cement covered with moss.

These topiary trees look very attractive standing at the entrance of the church or at the end of every third or fourth line of pews according to the space available.

COLUMNS

Columns are becoming very popular and are almost taking the place of pedestals. They are not as difficult to arrange as they would appear, and the container, or rather the 'construction' is easily made. You require a length of wood 2 in. (5 cm.) square which is set into a washing-up bowl containing cement to a depth of 2 in. (5 cm.). Attached to this by means of brackets are wooden platforms to hold the containers. The positioning of the platforms can be varied according to your requirements, with the final platform screwed securely to the top. The whole construction and your containers should be painted matt black or green. Holes can be drilled through corners of the platforms to enable wire to be threaded through tie your containers on. Take the wire over the foam and wire netting and tie it round the central pole. Water-retaining foam and/or wire netting is inserted on top of the cement at the base of the bowl.

An alternative construction can be made of metal, the central pole being screwed into a flat base for easy transportation and the top spiral being the correct size to take a cone (figure 20). The mechanics for both these constructions are concealed by your plant material in the lower holder covering the one above. It is advisable to recess one or two pieces of tall foliage at the start to cover up the pole.

Figure 20 Metal stand
Fourth tray placed at back of stand for depth/balance, and cone held at top by metal spiral attached to pole

These columns can be used very effectively either side of the altar, the screen or the entrance to the church and also against pillars. If possible, when standing them outside, it is advisable to tie them to the wall at some point to prevent them being blown over. Failing that, ensure the ground is flat, even if it means using a paving stone underneath them.

SPECIAL ARRANGEMENTS

Flowers are not always allowed on the altar and if the reredos is very ornate it may be more pleasing to stand pedestals or columns either side of the altar making sure they will not impede the movements of the clergy. In most churches, however, you can put flowers on the altar and you are able to design your festival so that the eye is drawn to the most important part of the church – the centre of worship – the altar.

When arrangements are designed to be placed on the altar, the overall line should be kept clear and simple using a few bold and distinct flowers such as lilies, carnations or achillea in preference to a variety of numerous small feathery varieties which will appear confused and be lost when seen from a distance. The colour must be luminous. White and gold always look right, and if you are matching the colour of the flowers with the colour of the altar frontal, either of these would be correct as the frontal used for festivals is invariably white or gold.

It is not unusual to be confronted with narrow-necked brass altar vases, designed originally to hold one stem of lilies, and which have been donated in memory of somebody. The use of an alternative is so undiplomatic as to be impossible. To help create a more pleasing outline than the neck would otherwise allow, place some water-retaining foam firmly into the top, allowing some of it to protrude above the rim. Cover it over with wire netting for additional anchorage, leaving a space in the foam at the back for watering. The flowers you use will be large and possibly heavy and the vase will be standing against the reredos so therefore most of the actual weight will be towards the front, and there is a danger of it overbalancing. To avoid this happening, a strip of lead should be hooked over the rim at the back, or a stone tied to the wire netting, acting as a counterbalance. Whatever you do, do not allow the flowers to come above the altar cross or in any way to overshadow it. Also make sure that they are not exactly the same height as the candles.

If it is possible to use an alternative container, a flat dish standing at the base of the altar cross, either behind or in front of it, with the candlesticks on either side, is a pleasing alternative. Keep the plant material low and wide. Great care should be taken of the linen cloth which should be covered with a piece of polythene before you begin to arrange.

It is always wise to consult the local priest or vicar about the positioning of flowers on the altar so they do not interfere with his ecclesiastical duties.

The pulpit

Many pulpits are highly decorated so anything other than a small arrangement is superfluous. It is often better to stand an arrangement at the bottom or at the side of the pulpit. A plaque or swag hanging on the wall above it may be sufficient, or such an arrangement may be hung on the front of the pulpit, attaching it to the wood with nylon fishing line.

The font

Plans for decorating the font should be fully discussed with the church authorities. Some allow flowers to be placed in the font giving the impression that the font is the container; others do not. Some allow flowers round the rim; others do not. The latter is very effective if kept simple, using small dainty unsophisticated flowers and foliage. These can be arranged either in a series of small tins (sardine tins disguised by being given a coat of matt grey paint) or in a tube of 1 in. (2.5 cm.) wire netting fashioned into shape and filled with damp sphagnum moss or wet foam, laid on thick polythene sheeting before the plant material is inserted. Do not place the flowers all the way round, leave a space for the clergy to use the font for the purpose for which it is intended. Whether there is a baptism during the festival or not, it should be possible to use the font if necessary.

If the font is used as the container, a plastic washing-up bowl is ideal to hold your plant material. You may need to raise it, as the font may be very deep. To make certain the inside is not scratched, a bowl can be reversed and then the other placed on top of it. You may be able to stand your arrangement on the top of the font having closed it with a lid. Whether the actual cover for the font is flat or not, it is advisable not to use it in case it is damaged by water spillage. It is better to make your own cover from a piece of wood which should be stained.

The choir stalls

These can inspire you with wonderful ideas but you should remember that choir stalls are functional. They are used by choristers wearing surplices, who may be little boys with inquisitive fingers and minds not always on the service. The floor is the best place for your flower arrangements – out of harm's way, and leading the eye up to the altar.

Plastic guttering makes ideal containers, cut to the required length with 'stops' at either end. Keep the arrangement fairly narrow to enable visitors and congregation to use the aisle without knocking against the plant material.

The aisle

Space is all-important here, especially if this is the main route for the visiting public as well as robed clergy and choir. Topiary trees, swags or pew ends are all possibilities, and should be attached firmly to the pews (figure 21).

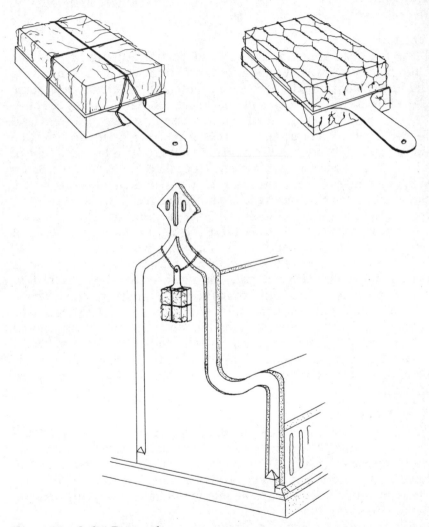

Figure 21 a & b Pew ends
Wreath trays using water-retaining foam covered in either thin plastic held by oasis tape or by chicken wire, and then suspended from the ends of the pews by wire or string

The pillars

Garlands have stood the test of time through many centuries and are still one of the nicest ways of embellishing the pillars. Swags and plaques of either fresh or dried plant material are an alternative.

The window sills

Unfortunately, many sills in churches slope downwards and no provision has been made to house a flower container. Well-soaked water-retaining foam wrapped in thin polythene, covered in wire netting and attached to the window with nylon fishing line is the easiest way of overcoming this problem. Or a container, such as a bread tin may be used with false legs glued to the front of it to make it level, and then tied to the window. Whatever type of mechanics you use, take advantage of the slope and have some of your plant material trailing down the sill.

If possible, it is better to place your arrangements at the sides of the windows regardless of whether they are of beautiful stained glass or plain. The lovely stone reveals are far better background than the windows.

If the windows are of stained glass, do not try to include every colour in your arrangement. Let one predominate and compliment the glass. Even with beautiful plant material you cannot and should not try to compete with the glass.

If the glass is plain, flowers are lost against the light, even when a backing of thick foliage is used, such as laurel or breech. Again, place your arrangements at the sides of the windows, following their architecture.

The radiators

Radiators can only be used in the summer when they are not giving out heat, and are best not used at all unless absolutely necessary. A bread tin may be tied securely to the top of each, and used as your container.

The porch

Flowers in the church porch give such a feeling of welcome, and there is usually room for an arrangement somewhere. Whatever style you decide on, it must be securely fixed and quite stable, because porches are very draughty places and do catch the wind.

Hanging baskets look charming suspended over the outer door, but they must be kept well sprayed as they tend to dry out very quickly, especially if it is sunny.

A large basket incorporating fruit and vegetables can be placed on the bench or a small cone could be stood on the window sill. Other alternatives are a garland over the church door or a plaque or swag of dried plant material resembling a Grinling Gibbons carving hung on the wall.

AFTER-CARE

Watering, topping-up and spraying are most important jobs and should be done thoroughly and carefully to avoid damage by water spillage. However well your plant material has been conditioned, it will drink avidly during the first 48 hours, and in churches moisture is drawn out of your containers and plant material by the dry atmosphere which stone walls create.

Nip or cut out any dead or wilting flowers or foliage. Do not attempt to pull it out as invariably something else comes with it and a larger gap than necessary results.

11. Drying and Preserving your Plant Material

Plant material which requires little after care and has so many uses is that which has been preserved with glycerine. It can be used most effectively in plaques and swags and also in arrangements which are staged too high to be watered. It can also be used in places where water is strictly forbidden, or when brown-coloured foliage is required for use with fresh plant material.

PRESERVING WITH GLYCERINE

Preserving means replacing the water in your plant material with glycerine, making it long-lasting, supple and pliable.

Mix together one part glycerine with two parts of hot water as this mixes with the glycerine better than cold, and the plant stems absorb it more quickly. Stir well. Cut away any damaged and crowded leaves and also the lower twigs of the foliage you want to preserve, and stand it in a jar containing no more than 1 in. (2.5 cm.) of the glycerine and water solution. More can be added later. It is advisable to use a clear glass jar enabling you to keep a careful watch on the level of solution so that you can top it up when necessary. Scrape the bark from any woody stems and split them with a knife.

Do not leave it too late in the year before gathering your foliage. Pick it before its colour begins to turn – June, July and August are the best months. It is equally important not to collect it when it is too young; it must be mature, otherwise it does not absorb the solution. The length of time your plant material should be left in the glycerine varies from a few days to a few weeks. Remove it when it has changed colour. If it is left too long in the solution and drops of glycerine appear on the leaves, do not worry, simply swish it in detergent and water, and then hang it out to dry. Wipe the ends of the stems and either hang them up or store in a dry place in boxes, but do not keep them in polythene bags as they will become mildewed. A variety of shades of colour in the same plant material may be obtained by standing some of the stems in the sun which will turn them much lighter.

The following plants are particularly useful and can be successfully preserved:

Aspidistra	Broom	Camellia
Beech	Dock	Fatsia japonica
Box	Grevillia	Laurel
Choisya	Molucella	Oak
Fiscus (Rubber Plant)	Mahonia	Pampas Grass
	Skimmia	

It is an advantage to mop the leaves of the aspidistra, fatsia and fiscus on both sides with the solution before standing the stems in the glycerine. It is also advantageous to stand seed heads in the solution making them far less brittle than when allowing to dry. The seed heads of foxgloves – old mans' beard (remove leaves) – angelica – verbascum – montbretia – nigella – nicandra and dock are all suitable.

Drying plant material
Dried plant material is more fragile than plant material which has been preserved with glycerine, and should be handled and stored carefully.

Pick perfect flowers on a dry day. Remove all the leaves because they shrivel. Tie into small bunches using elastic bands rather then string or wire. The elastic tightens as the stems shrink and prevents them from falling out of the bunch. Hang in bunches in a dry, airy place such as in the garage or near the boiler. Hanging gives a better shape to the plants than leaving them in jars where they tend to droop. Store in boxes or in upright jars if they are likely to be squashed.

Materials which dry very successfully by this method include acanthus, achillea, cardoons Chinese lanterns (*physalis*), dock echinops, eryngium, hydrangea, sedum and teazel. Grasses and bullrushes may be sprayed with hair lacquer to prevent them from exploding. Hydrangeas may be dried by standing them in 2 in. (5 cm.) of water as soon as the heads feel papery on the plant, and leaving them until the water has evaporated. They may also stand in the glycerine solution.

If, after drying them you wish to use your plant material in water, dip the end of the stems in candle wax or nail polish to seal. Dry them thoroughly before re-storing. It is also possible to dry plant material with desiccants such as silicagel, borax or sand, which preserves the colours. Spring flowers are particularly suitable for treatment, and may be used in garlands, plaques and swags. Bookmarks used on the lectern can be decorated with smaller plants dried in this manner, and they may also be used to enhance the advertisements you put in hotels, libraries and shops to publicize your show or festival.

HOW AND WHEN TO DRY PLANTS

A Stark Stem	Stand upright and well-spaced in a jar to allow air to circulate.
B Weak Stem	Strip off the leaves and hang heads downwards in small bunches. Leave in a dry, dark room which should be warm, not hot.
C	Cut off stalks 2 in. (5 cm.) from flower head. Place a layer of borax in a box and insert the stalks carefully until the back of the flower is resting on the borax. Gently shake the borax all round and in between each petal. Leave two weeks and then check.
D	Leave on plant as long as possible. Finish drying indoors by standing stalks in 2 in. (5 cm.) of water until all water has gone.
E	Coloured leaves. Press between sheets of blotting paper under carpet or between heavy books.
F	Preserved with glycerine.

When to Harvest

X	When last buds are showing colour.
Y	When first buds are showing colour.
Z	In full bloom.
W	When seed heads are open.
V	When seed heads are ripe.
U	Watch the leaves.

TABLE OF DRYING METHODS
AND HARVESTING TIMES

Flowers			Foliage		
Achillea	A	Z	Aquilegia	E	
Allium	C	X	Beech	F	July & September
Amaranthus	B	X		E	September
Anaphalis	B	Z	Bracken	E	under carpet at least two months
Anemones	C early	Z			
Buddleia	A	X	Laurel	F	any time
Daffodils	C	X	Mahonia	E	
Delphiniums	B	X	Maidenhair fern	E	
Echiniops (var)	A	Y	Oak	F	when leaves are coloured but veins are green
Hydrangea	D		Eucalyptus	F	winter
Larkspur	A	Y	Fern	E	under carpet for at least two months
Marigold	C early	Z			
Mimosa	B	Z	Grevillea	F	winter
Pansy	E	X	Hawthorn	F	when flush appears over tree
Paeonies	C early	Z	Hosta	D	
Ranunculas	C early	Z	Sweet chestnut	E	any time
Roses	C early	Z	Viburnum (Gelder rose)	F	
Salvia	D	L			
Solidago	B	X			
Tansy	A	X			
Violas	X				
Pussy willow	A	Y			
Zinnia	C early	Z			

12. Growing for Shows

An entire book could be and indeed has been devoted to the plant material which all keen flower arrangers should grow. The list is endless and we all have our favourites, but plant material grown for show work must have one essential quality. It must be long-lasting and be able to stand for three to four days. Nothing is more depressing than to see wilted exhibits on the last day of the show or flower festival.

Plant material is divided into three basic categories: outline material which is fine or pointed; the rounder, more solid shapes for the centre of interest and to give weight; and the transitional or 'in-between' shapes which graduate from the fine to the solid.

Listed below is a selection of plants which will last well when cut. By each entry is marked the category into which it falls, together with its dominant characteristic, e.g., its splendid spikes of flowers, or the colour of its foliage in autumn. Growing instructions have been kept to a minimum, only the particular plant's preference for sun or shade is stated.

TABLE OF PLANTS

Sh shrub; **P** perennial; **A** annual; **D** dry; **G** glycerine; **O** outline; **R** round; **T** transitional.

Name	Type of Plant	Position	Preserve	Shape
Abelia grandiflora (Sh)	bronze-pink bracts;	sun		T
	bright green, pointed leaves			O
Acanthus mollis (P)	purplish flower spikes;	sun/shade	D	O
	large shiny leaves; use			
	when mature			
Achillea 'Gold Plate' (P)	flat yellow flower heads	sun	D	R
Aconitum carmichaelii (P)	racemes of purple flowers	semi shade	D	O
lycoctonum (P)	racemes of lime green		D	O
	flowers			
Alchemilla mollis (P)	lime green flowers;	sun/shade	D & G	T
	round hairy leaves		G	R

Name	Type of Plant	Position	Preserve	Shape
Alstromeria ligtu (P)	pink, lilac and yellow flowers	sun		O & T
Amaranthus caudatus 'Viridus' (A)	green pendulous flowers	sun	D	
Angelica (P)	large green flower heads: use when mature; light green leaves	sun	D	R R
Arum italicum pictum (P)	glossy, veined leaves	damp/shade		R
Aruncus sylvester (P)	feathery cream flower spikes; light green lanceolate leaflets	sun/shade	D	
Astilbe arendsii (P)	pointed plumes of white, pink and red; mid green divided leaves	sun/shade	D	O T
Astrantia major (P)	greenish pink flowers: use on short stem; mid green leaves	shade	D & G	
Aucuba japonica (Sh)	shiny green leaves mottled cream	sun/shade		R & T
Bergenia cordifolia (P)	heads of lilac rose flowers; round, mid-green leaves	sun/shade		R & T R
Berberis thunbergii atropurpura (Sh)	yellow flowers; purple: leaves: take out tip of spray	sun/shade		O O
Buxus sempervirens aureo-maculata (Sh)	variegated green and yellow	sun/shade	G	O
Camellia japonica (Sh)	pink, red and white flowers; dark glossy leaves	shelter	G	O & T O & T
Campanula glomerata superba (P)	deep violet flowers	sun		O
Cassinia fulvida (Sh)	small white flowers; yellow/green leaves	sun		T T
Choisya ternata (Sh)	white flowers; dark green glossy leaves	sun/shade	G	T & R
Cimicifuga racemosa (Bugsbane) (P)	plumes of creamy flowers; fern-like leaves	shade		O T
Cobaea scandens	purple or green/white flowers	sun		T & R
Crocosmia crocosmiflora (P)	orange flowers; sword-like leaves	sun	D D	O O
Cupressus, various (tree)	fern-like foliage	sun/shade	G	T
Cynara cardunculus (P)	seed head; large grey leaves	sun/shade	D	R R
Dahlia, various	flowers of many different colours	sun		T & R
Delphinium, various (P)	white, blue and mauve spikes	sun	D	O
Dianthus caryophyllus (P)	white, pink and red flowers	sun		T & R

Name	Type of Plant	Position	Preserve	Shape
Eleagnus marophylla (Sh)	green leaves backed with grey	sun/shade	G	O & T
Escallonia, various (Sh)	pink and red flowers; mid to deep green glossy lanceolate leaves	sun/shade	G	O / O
Eucalyptus perriniana (tree)	grey orbicular leaves	sun/shade	G	O
Euphorbia polychroma (P)	yellow flowers	sun		T & R
robbiae (P)	lime green flowers; rosette leaves			T
griffithii 'Fireglow'	orange flowers			T & R
Fatsia japonica (Sh)	large glossy leaves	shelter	G	R
Garrya elliptica (Sh)	yellow catkins; dark green leaves	sun/shade	G / G	O / O & T
Gladiolus primulinus and butterfly	various colours	sun		O
Hedra, various	trailing foliage	sun/shade		O
Helleborus, various (P)	green, pink and mauve flowers use only when mature; dark green lanceolate and lobed leaves	shade	G	T / R & T
Hosta, various (P)	pale mauve and white flowers; but grown for the green, yellow and grey-green leaves; seed heads will dry	shade	D / Press	O / R
Ilex acquifolium 'Golden Queen' (Sh)	berries; variegated leaves	sun/shade		O & T
Iris pallida dalmatica (P)	lavender flowers; green grey strap leaves	sun		O
Jasminum nudiflorum	yellow flowers; small dark green leaves	sun/shade		O / O
Kniphofia uvaria (P)	red/yellow flowers	sun		O
Ligustrum ovalifolum aureum (Golden Privet) (Sh)	yellow, green-flecked leaves	sun/shade		O
Macleaya cordata (P)	pearly-white flowers: cut when mature; bronze, backed with grey leaves	sun		O / R
Mahonia, various (Sh)	yellow flowers; also berries; dark green, spine-toothed leaves	sun/shade	G	O & T / T
Molucella laevis (A)	shell-like, pale green calyx	sun	G & D	O
Nicotiana alata (A)	green, white and pink flowers	sun		O & T
Osmunda regalis (Fern)	pea green leaves	shade	Press	O & T
Paeonia, various (P)	white, pink and red flowers; green leaves with good autumn colouring	sun	Press	R / T & R

115

Name	Type of Plant	Position	Preserve	Shape
Phlomis fruiticosa (P)	yellow flowers; interesting seed head	sun	D	O
Phormium tenax atropurpureum (P)	bronze strap leaves	sun		O
Pieris formosa (Sh)	white flowers leaves of red turning to green	sun/shade		O T & R
Polygonatum multiflorum (P)	white flowers; mid green leaves, arching stem	shade	G	O
Senecio areyi (Sh)	grey felted leaves	sun/shade		O & T
Skimmia rubella (Sh)	pink flowers	sun/shade		T
japonica (Sh)	white flowers and red berries; dark green obovate leaves		G	T & R
Stephanandra tanakae (Sh)	leaves of mid green turning to deep yellow on long arching branches	sun/shade		O O
Tellima grandiflora (P)	green bell flowers tipped with pink; green leaves tinged with pink, turning to bronze	sun/shade		O R
Verbascum broussa (P)	spikes of yellow flowers	sun	D	O
Viburnum opulus sterile (Sh)	green flowers turning to white; green maple-like leaves turning to red in autumn	sun		T & R O & T
Vinca major elegantissima (P)	variegated leaves on trailing stems	shade		O
Weigela florida variegata (Sh)	pink flowers variegated leaves on arching stems	sun		O
Yucca flaccida (Sh)	yellowish white flowers;	sun		O
Zinnia 'Envy' (A)	lime green flowers	sun		R

VARIETIES OF ROSES

Roses are superb for flower arranging. They have a quality all of their own. They can be used in any style of arrangement from period to modern, and look equally good arranged in a glass, silver or pewter container, or with driftwood. They look beautiful on their own but will mix happily with any other flowers, often providing 'in-between' colour which ties an arrangement together.

Although many good varieties are obtainable from the florist, the much sought after, unusual colourings are to be found only in gardens. Some of the names listed below are given with that in mind.

F floribunda; **HT** hybrid tea; **Sh** shrub.
Amberlight (F) orange/brown
Artistic (F) golden brown
Blessings (F) coral/pink
Brownie (F) pinky/brown
Constance Spry (Sh) pink
Elizabeth of Glamis (F) light salmon/orange
Fred Gibson (HT) yellow to apricot
Green Diamond (sometimes called Greensleeves) (F) pink turning
to green
Iceberg (F) white
Iced Ginger (F) ivory to copper
Jocelyn (F) brown/purple
Julia (HT) coppery parchment
Just Joey (HT) coppery orange
Magenta (Sh) rosy magenta
Pierre Oger (Bourbon) blush pink
Rosemary Rose (F) bright carmine red
Tom Brown (F) two-tone brown
Tynewald (F) ivory to buff
Vesper (F) orange/brown
Whisky Mac (HT) deep gold with bronze

A rose to be grown not for its flowers but for its foliage and lovely hips is Rosa rubrifolia. It has long arching branches of silvery-purple leaves which blend with any colour scheme.

13. How to Develop your Interest in Flower Arranging

If your interest in flower arranging has been stimulated and you wish to develop it further, there are various paths which you may follow depending on the amount of free time and how thoroughly you wish to study flower arranging and its allied subjects, such as botany and horticulture.

JOINING A FLOWER CLUB

Throughout Great Britain there are some 100,000 men and women who are members of the 1,400 flower clubs affiliated to the National Association of Flower Arrangement Societies of Great Britain (NAFAS). NAFAS is the official organization for British flower arrangers, and for administrative purposes its 1,400 clubs are divided into 20 geographical areas. Judges, demonstrators and speakers are trained and tested to a very high standard, and the education committee of the association runs a very flourishing teachers' association. Residential conferences and courses on every conceivable subject allied to flower arranging are organized each year, as well as competitive shows and exhibitions at club, area and national levels.

In most towns and many villages there exists a flourishing flower club. Wherever you live there is likely to be one near you, and if you would like details of your nearest club and when it meets, write to NAFAS and the association will be happy to supply all the information you require.

Nearly all clubs hold their meetings monthly, either in the afternoon or evening, and their size can vary from 30 to 300 members. The meetings consist of a demonstration by a visiting qualified demonstrator or, occasionally, a speaker on allied subjects, who may illustrate her talk with slides. A competition with a different theme or title each month may also be included. Members may, if they wish, bring an exhibit to be judged, and receive constructive comments on their work, thus helping them to improve month by month.

All clubs run a flower arranging accessory sales table stocked with the necessary mechanics such as pinholders, candle cups, cones, water-retaining foam, oasis tape, wires, etc. and perhaps a selection of bases, baskets, containers, Christmas accessories and ribbons, all to be purchased at very reasonable prices. They may also run a plant stall and a library, and of course the very informative instruction leaflets and booklets published by NAFAS will be on sale. These cover such subjects as *Care of Cut Flowers*; *Preserving Plant Material*; *Use of Driftwood*; *Pressed Flower Pictures*; *Swags and Plaques*; *Home-made Containers*; *Figurines*, and many other useful titles.

In addition to the monthly meetings a number of classes may be run for beginners. Day schools may be held on particular subjects such as 'Modern and abstract work'; 'Swags, collage and plaques'; 'Interpretative flower arranging'; and 'Show work'. Competitive shows are held once or sometimes twice a year, and it is here where you can begin to discover the pleasures and excitement of competing, progressing from the monthly competitions to club shows, then to the larger county and area shows, and eventually to the large horticultural shows and the annual national competition staged in a different part of the country each year by NAFAS. Here, as a competitor or one of the organizing committee you cannot fail to improve your standard and gain not only a wealth of knowledge but lasting friendship from your fellow members.

Non-competitive shows and exhibitions may also be part of a club's programme. Very many local churches throughout the country have held most successful and profitable festivals of flowers which have been organized by their flower clubs. Exhibitions have been held in many beautiful stately homes; churches and cathedrals. Whilst members of lower clubs derive great pleasure from these many aspects of their hobby, they have the added satisfaction of knowing that they have also raised over two million pounds for various charities.

It is through a flower club, the area newsletter or the quarterly magazine, *The Flower Arranger*, published by NAFAS, that you hear about all the other activities in the flower arranging world in which you can take part both locally and nationally.

CORRESPONDENCE COURSES

Although flower arranging is essentially a practical subject, those who, because of family commitments, full-time working hours or geographical isolation, are prevented from attending flower-arranging meetings or classes, may wish to take advantage of a correspondence course. NAFAS has devised a course consisting of ten lessons which provide a firm basis for practical work, further study and experiment, enabling students to work at their own pace and in their own homes.

FLOWER ARRANGING

Classes in flower arrangement are usually available in every area, most often held by the local authority at centres of adult education in purpose-built centres or schools. Other classes are held by women's organizations or church or craft groups for their members. A list of qualified teachers is available from NAFAS, and additional information can be given to those wishing to join or start a class. Non-vocational classes, i.e. those without an examination at the end, may be of short duration, from between six to 12 weeks, or they may last for three terms. A short course will cover the use of mechanics, that is, the means by which plant material is held in position; the selection of suitable plant material; the preparation of flowers and foliage so that it will last when arranged; and the use of simple containers that may be found around the home.

A longer course gives scope for creativity and an awareness of the materials that nature provides. Students may study the design qualities of weathered wood, bark, fungi, shells, stones, seedheads and other materials that may be found on a country walk or sea-shore scavenging. Drying and preserving plant material for winter use is an important part of the flower arranger's year, and this skill is usually covered during a longer course. Students may be shown how to press plant material to make pressed flower pictures or cards, a craft revived from Victorian times.

Flower arranging and gardening go hand in hand, and the growing of one's own material is a pleasurable task. Advice will be given on the growing of plants from seeds and cuttings.

CITY AND GUILDS OF LONDON INSTITUTE

The examination course run by the City of Guilds of London Institute offers even wider horizons and greater interest. The course is designed for beginners as well as for those who already have some knowledge of the subject. Creativity is an important facet, and this is exemplified by the common core syllabus which aims to develop a creative approach to the subject to stimulate ideas.

Part 1 is taken over a two-year period. This usually means one day or two evenings a week at a college of further education or a horticultural institute. The syllabus covers basic skills, the application in flower arrangement of the design principles and elements, designs for specific settings, seasons and occasions, show work, botany, horticulture and photography. There is an examination at the end of the second year.

Part 2 lasts one year and covers the history of flower arrangement, abstract style and its relationship with other art forms, exhibition work, show work and judging, greenhouse gardening, garden design and botany. The history of flower arrangement includes the use of flowers and foliage by ancient civilizations; types of containers suitable for period arrangements; room settings; plant material used decoratively on furnishings; and gardens laid out in the style of an earlier century. The subject matter can suggest many other topics of study. A glimpse of a delicate pomander on display in a stately home can spark off an interest in herbs and herb gardens. A museum collection of delicate Chinese porcelain can give rise to an investigation into the symbolic use of plants in Ancient China. Often course students are invited to stage a flower festival or to put up an exhibition at a flower show.

The examination at the end of Part 2 is the craft qualification necessary before going on to take a Further Education Teacher's Certificate. Many students feel a great sense of achievement at having tackled the course, and go on to become flower arrangement demonstrators, judges or club officers.

Glossary of terms used in flower arranging

Abstract: Plant material used in a way which does not relate to its normal growth habit and where design qualities predominate.

Accessory: Articles other than base, background, container and drapes used with your plant material in an exhibit.

Annual: A plant that lives only one year.

Asymmetrical: An exhibit in which plant material is not identical in shape or size on either sides of an imaginary central line, the balance being achieved by equal visual weight.

Background: A material backing of fabric, hardboard or covered wood, etc., placed behind an exhibit by the committee or competitor to improve its appearance.

Balance: Balance can be asymmetrical or symmetrical – visual or actual. Actual balance is the steadiness or firmness of the plant material. Visual balance is the equality of weight either side of an imaginary central line.

Base: A base is anything on which your exhibit stands and can be made of any material except artificial grass.

Bract: A leaf-like part at the base of a flower which, in NAFAS shows, may be used as either flowers or foliage.

Collage: A collage is made predominately or entirely of plant material which is attached to a framed or unframed background.

Conditioning: Conditioning means doing whatever is necessary to ensure cut plant material absorbs as much moisture as possible before it is arranged to prevent wilting and to prolong its life.

Cone: a A container made of metal or plastic used to give additional height either to the arrangement or to shorter plant material.

   b A style of decoration where plant material is fashioned into the shape of a cone.

Container: A container is anything in which plant material can be arranged. When fresh plant material is used, it must be able to hold water or water-retaining foam.

Drape: A piece of fabric placed behind or used in association with an exhibit.

Driftwood: Any kind of weathered wood including bark, branches or roots.

Exhibit: Plant material, with or without accessories, contained within a space as specified in the show schedule.

Festival of flowers: The time when a stately home, church or cathedral is decorated with flowers and is open to the public.

Figurines: One or more figures on a single base. If not used as the container for plant material it is considered an accessory.

Focal point: The centre of interest in a flower arrangement, and the point to which your eye is immediately drawn. It is usually at the base of the tallest stem.

Garland: Plant material bound on to rope or inserted into water-retaining foam to form a long flexible strip.

Interpreting: Using the plant material to depict the title of the class; if allowed and desired, this may be assisted by the discriminate use of accessories.

Mechanics: The equipment used to hold your plant material in position, ie, pinholder, water-retaining foam, wire netting.

Miniature: An exhibit which is not more than 4 in. (10 cm.) in height, width or depth, ie, would fit easily into a 4 in. cube.

Niche: An alcove or recess in which an exhibit may be placed.

Perennial: A plant which comes up again year after year.

Petite: An exhibit which is more than 4 in. (10 cm.) but less than 9 in. (23 cm.) in width, depth and height.

Pinholder: This is used to hold plant material in position. It has a heavy metal base with protruding spikes.

Plaque: See Collage.

Pleats: Knife pleats are parallel pleats, the edges of which all fall in the same direction.

      Box pleats are pleats that stand out on the right side of the material, with the two edges of one pleat facing in opposite directions.

Pot-et-fleur: Cut flowers and growing plants, in or out of their pots, arranged together in one container. Accessories are permitted, but not cut foliage.

Predominate: To be present in greater quantity or be stronger visually than the rest of the materials used.

Schedule: The paper on which is listed details and requirements for all classes of exhibits in a flower show.

Space: The area allocated for each exhibit. No exhibit should exceed the given space or touch the sides of the niche.

Staging: (a) The putting up of an exhibit by a competitor or

      (b) the tables, platforms, benches, stands, alcoves, niches etc. and their coverings, on which the exhibits are displayed.

Swag: This is made predominately or entirely with plant material without a visible background.

Symmetrical: An exhibit where the size, shape and depth of colour of the plant material are equal on either side of an imaginary central line.

Transition: The plant material used to bring about a gradual change in an exhibit from fine outline to the heavier centre, or from one colour to another.

Velcro: A commercial product for fastening two surfaces together. It is made in two sections, one with a velvet finish and the other with a hooked surface, and these adhere when pressed together.

Water-retaining foam: The substance which holds the cut ends of plant material in position.

Wire: The higher the gauge number, the finer the wire. Wire used in flower arranging varies from 16-gauge to 36-gauge.

Metric conversion table

	Metres	Centimetres
1 inch		2.54
2 inches		5.08
3 inches		7.62
4 inches		10.16
5 inches		12.70
6 inches		15.24
7 inches		17.78
8 inches		20.32
9 inches		22.86
10 inches		25.40
11 inches		27.94
12 inches	0.30	30.48
2 feet	0.61	60.96
3 feet	0.91	91.44
4 feet	1.22	121.90
5 feet	1.52	152.40
6 feet	1.83	182.90
7 feet	2.13	213.30
8 feet	2.43	243.80

Direct conversions of specific sizes given in this book have been made to the nearest centimetre.

Useful addresses

INFORMATION

National Association of Flower Arrangement Societies of Great Britain (NAFAS), 21a Denbigh Street, London, SW1V 2HF
The National Council of State Garden Clubs Inc. (NCSGC), 4401 Magnolia Avenue, St. Louis, Missouri 63110
The National Federation of Women's Institutes, 39 Eccleston Street, London, SW1W 9NT
City & Guilds of London Institute, 46 Britannia Street, London WC1
The Royal Horticultural Society, Vincent Square, London, SW1P 2PE

CONTAINERS

Wrought iron pedestals, bases, containers, turntables, etc.

Jon Eversfield Metal Products, 62 Paterson Place, Shepshed, Leicestershire.

Osmington Forge, Osmington, Near Weymouth, Dorset, DT3 6EN
Richard Quinnell Limited, Rowhurst Forge, Oxshott Road, Leatherhead, Surrey.

Pottery

Clive Brooker, Stanmore Pottery, 10 York Avenue, Stanmore, Middlesex, HA7 2HS
Joyce Withey, Bumbles, Moreton Road, Ongar, Essex.

PLANTS

Bulbs

Walter Blom & Son Ltd., Coombelands Nurseries, Leavesden, Watford, Herts, WD2 7BH
van Turbergen Limited, Willow Bank Wharf, Ranelegh Gardens, Fulham, London, SW6

Herbaceous Plants

Beth Chatto, Whitebarn House, Elmstead Market, Colchester CO7 7DB
Kelways Nurseries, Langport, Somerset TA10 95L

Roses

Le Grice roses, Norwich Road, North Walsham, Norfolk, NR28 0DR
John Mattock Ltd., The Rose Nurseries, Nuneham Courteney, Oxford.

Shrubs

Notcutt's Nurseries, Woodbridge, Suffolk.
South Down Nurseries, Southgate Street, Redruth, Cornwall.

STAGING MATERIALS

J.W. Bollom & Co. Ltd, Croydon Road, Elmers End, Beckenham, Kent, BR3 4BL (*Felt, hessian and display drapes*)
B. Brown (Holborn) Ltd, 32/33 Greville Street, London EC1N 8TD (*Felt, display drape, display suede, hessian, casement and muslin*)
Cavalcade Fabric, 189 Muster Road, London SW6 6BZ (*Jersey and nylon jersey*)
J & P Display Ltd, 10 Greystoke Court, Hanger Lane, London W5 1EN (*Display aids, drawing pins, and staples*)
The Eaton Bag Co., 16 Manette Street, London W1 (*Shells, cane, raffia, straw matting and bamboo*)
Graphex Industrial Art Ltd, 51 Lisson Grove, London NW1 6UJ (*Letters and lettering including cork and self-adhering plastic*)
Limericks (Linens) Ltd, 117 Victoria Avenue, Southend-on-Sea, Essex, SS2 6EL (*Polyester/cotton sheeting, cambric, hessian*)

Paper

B. Garrard Ltd, Water Lane, King's Langley, Herts. (*Corrugated paper and niches*)
Leete & Co. Ltd, The Grange, Pickmere, Nr. Knutsford, Cheshire. (*Corrugated cardboard*)
Paperchase, Tottenham Court Road, London, WC1. (*Everything in paper*)

WHOLESALERS AND MANUFACTURERS IN THE USA

Barry David Fabrics Co., 155 Sixth Street, Chelsea, Massachusetts.
Harrison Textiles, 31 Harrison Avenue, Boston, Massachusetts.
Sumner Katz & Co., 75/85 Kneeland Street, Boston, Massachusetts.
Schmacher, 939 Third Avenue, New York 10022.
Charles H. Steward & Co., 8 Clarendon Street, Sommerville, Massachusetts.

Recommended reading

AARONSON, Marian, *The Art of Flower Arranging*, Grower Books, 1970; *Design with Plant Material*, Grower Books, 1972.
EMBERTON, Sybil, *Garden Foliage for Flower Arrangement*, Faber & Faber, 1968; *Shrub Gardening for Flower Arrangement*, Faber & Faber 1965.
HAY, Roy and SYNGE, Patrick, *The Dictionary of Garden Plants in Colour*, Michael Joseph, 1976.
MACQUEEN, Sheila, *Encyclopaedia of Flower Arrangement*, Faber & Faber, 1969.
NAFAS,*The Flower Arranger* (quarterly magazine); *Guide to Church Flowers; Guide to Period Flower Arranging; Handbook of Schedule Definitions; Judges' Manual*; various instruction leaflets.
TAYLOR, Jean, *Practical Flower Arranging*, Hamlyn, 1974; *Creative Flower Arrangement*, Stanley Paul, 1973; *Flowers in Church*, Mowbray, 1976.
VAGG, Daphne, *Flower Arranging*, Ward Lock, 1980; *Flowers for the Table*, Batsford, 1983; *Flower Arranging through the Year*, Batsford, 1983.
WEBB, Iris, *The Complete Guide to Flower and Foliage Arrangement*, Webb & Bower, 1979.
Flora published every two months by Stanley Gibbons Magazines, Drury House, Russell Street, London, WC2B 5HD.

Index

This index does not include plants whose names occur on pages 69-70 and 113-16 only.